4 CHRONIC DISORDERS, DISEASES, AND SYNDROMES DEMYSTIFIED

A PROVEN FIVE-STEP, SIMPLE TO UNDERSTAND, AND EASY TO IMPLEMENT SELF-HEALING GUIDE TO PREVENT, TREAT, AND POSSIBLY REVERSE DIGESTIVE TRACT CONDITIONS, INCLUDING GUT, INFLAMMATORY, AND AUTOIMMUNE DISORDERS, DISEASES, AND CHRONIC PAIN SYNDROME BY MAKING SIMPLE LIFESTYLE CHANGES

DR SHAHID SHEIKH

CONTENTS

To my wife, Fatima Husain, MD,
Your unwavering love and steadfast support have been my anchor through the highs and lows of life. This book is a tribute to your enduring presence in my life, and I dedicate this book to you with all my love and gratitude.

Trigger warning: This book discusses and describes many chronic diseases that may upset some readers.

INTRODUCTION

Half of all Americans are suffering from some form of chronic disease or pain at this very moment. A quarter of these will be suffering from multiple chronic diseases. Chronic diseases—diseases that last longer than three months—result in 75% of all deaths yearly (The Silver Book, n.d.). Many chronic diseases—such as cancer, diabetes, arthritis, etc.—can be managed for years and, in several cases, are never cured but managed for life. These diseases not only place a physical, mental, and emotional strain on the sufferer but can devastate families and loved ones with the strain and cost of treatment.

Although there are numerous medical systems available to the public, the most widely practiced systems are allopathy (also known as modern medicine, mainstream medicine, biomedicine, Western medicine, conventional medicine, or orthodox medicine), ayurvedic, homeopathy, traditional Chinese medicine (TCM), and naturopathy. While modern medicine has come a long way, it has its shortcomings; one of which is that it is designed and taught in medical schools to manage only symptoms, not treat or cure the underlying causes.

Chronic diseases and pain cause people to feel as if they're losing control of their lives due to the unpredictability of their vastly life-limiting symptoms. For others, the increasingly high financial cost of treatment and management of chronic problems is a burden they can't handle—especially when the condition prevents them from working, making them feel more stressed and spiking their anxiety.

Many chronic disease and pain sufferers are becoming frustrated with the traditional medical systems not offering the relief they promise. The symptoms associated with chronic diseases put a damper on life due to the physical limitations and discomfort they bring, as pain and fatigue can lead to mobility problems. These symptoms also drain a person emotionally, socially, and financially, causing damage to their identity and self-worth. People are often identified by what they're suffering from, diminishing their humanity. This emotional toll leads to a lower quality of life, which can bring about depression.

Perhaps you are suffering from a chronic disease, pain, or both. Likely, you are tired of illness and pain, seeing no end to this black hole that swallows up your time, health, and money. All you want is relief! You may have convinced yourself there's no relief and you have to learn to live with it. However, you're holding the key to relief from chronic diseases and pain in your very hands.

You don't need to suffer through debilitating symptoms when you can live your life to the fullest. Being diagnosed with a chronic disease or suffering from chronic pain doesn't have to be the end of your life. I recall a story of an acquaintance, Markus, who lived his life to the fullest until he started having kidney trouble in 2015. After several tests, his doctors found his kidneys were in the early stages of failure, and at first, the doctors had no idea why. Eventually, Markus was diagnosed with systemic lupus erythematosus, also known as lupus. This disease is incurable and can only be managed. What made this diagnosis worse was that he was diagnosed with lupus nephritis as well, meaning the condition was also targeting his kidneys. Equipped with knowledge about the disease, Markus made a few simple lifestyle changes. He switched to a plant-based diet, eliminated processed foods, and lowered his sodium intake to protect his kidneys and help with his high blood pressure. Markus now prefers to eat fish for his protein, enjoys fresh fruits and vegetables, and consumes berries as his new candy. He had to make other changes, including drinking more water, getting more sleep, learning to relax, and exercising. These changes took time, but by making them, he ensured he could live longer, healthier, and more comfortably.

I have spent the last 50 years suffering from chronic diseases and pain. It all started with a night parachute jump in 1974, which just about destroyed my lower back. No one could help me, and most doctors addressed the symptoms and not the cause, prescribing more potent painkillers and opiates every time I complained of pain.

Subsequently, when doctors failed to diagnose the cause(s) of my debilitating pain, they thought that I may have fibromyalgia or perhaps depression and prescribed antibiotics, steroids, antidepressants, and an array of other medications, which resulted in chronic weight gain, type 2 diabetes, and high blood pressure.

In 1999, an acquaintance gave me a gift of a pair of hand-raised Cockatiels who, I soon found out, made great, charming, and entertaining companions. I enjoyed their company so much that I began to acquire other similar species of birds, mostly parrots—over a hundred in a very short period. However, I soon began to experience sporadic severe respiratory symptoms, including unexplained bouts of continuous coughing, shortness of breath, muscle aches, high fever, chills, unexplained tiredness, lack of energy, and body pains.

In late 1999, I returned to the doctors in general/family practice, who, not understanding the causes, began treating the symptoms with over-the-counter nonsteroidal anti-inflammatory drugs (NSAIDs) and cough syrup. After six months of suffering and frustration with the lack of proper diagnosis and solutions to my illnesses, I found a pulmonary medicine group practice comprised of specialists in rare pulmonary specialty pulmonary medicine, idiopathic pulmonary fibrosis, pulmonary fibrosis, interstitial lung disease, mycobacterial lung disease, and hypersensitivity where a pulmonologist specializing in rare diseases determined that I had bird fancier's pneumonitis, a rare lung disease known as hypersensitivity pneumonitis, an immunologically mediated lung disease due to repetitive exposure to airborne avian antigens.

The doctor prescribed very high doses of antibiotics and steroids to suppress the symptoms. Sadly, this destroyed my digestive system and wouldn't be the last time I would be misdiagnosed.

In 2010, while on a leadership coaching assignment in Asia, I began to experience tremors and weakness in my legs, often falling. I immediately returned to the US to consult with a neurologist. After a battery of physical tests and lab work, I was misdiagnosed with either multiple sclerosis (MS)—a progressive disease of the central nervous system—or amyotrophic lateral sclerosis (ALS)—a progressive neurodegenerative disease that affects nerve cells in the brain and spinal cord. Later, other doctors believed I had inclusion body myositis (IBM), another inflammatory condition that causes muscle weakness. Since IBM closely mimics MS, my doctors weren't sure which I had at first. After more tests and more meds than I could count, I finally got an answer that I didn't expect: Parkinson's disease.

It didn't matter what my diagnosis was in the end. Everything the doctors gave me only treated my symptoms and never got to the root of my problems. I was sick and tired of being let down by modern medicine. I needed to take my health into my own hands. For the past ten years, I have been educating myself about traditional and alternative medicines to see how to help myself best. I researched, read everything I could find, and attended many online courses and webinars. Some of these courses covered mindfulness, meditation, food as medicine, nutrition, self-awareness, and even pain management. I spent so much time in my research that I ended up with a long list of certifications, some of which included:

- Mindful Awareness Practice
- Social + Emotional Intelligence Assessment Practitioner
- Foundational Skills of Emotional Intelligence (Daniel Goleman)
- The Power of Awareness
- Mindfulness Meditation Teacher Certification Program
- Food as Medicine
- Chronic Pain Management
- How to Mend the Leaky Gut
- And many more

By the end of my research and experimenting with various holistic methods, I discovered the five-step healing guide—the Holistic Transformation Method adapted from the work of James Samuel Gordon in his book *The Transformation: Discovering Wholeness and Healing After Trauma.* Helping you heal from chronic disease and pain is as easy as the following steps:

1. **Discover:** Learn about your condition and its contributing factors.
2. **Eliminate:** Remove food triggers from your diet.
3. **Nourish:** Consume nutrient-dense whole foods that support the healing process.
4. **Enhance:** Incorporate specific supplements to optimize healing.
5. **Balance:** Cultivate mindfulness and awareness to support overall wellness.

Armed with the knowledge I had accumulated and this five-step program, I worked hard to manage my disorders and adopted a healthy lifestyle. Thanks to my persistence, I dropped 72 pounds, reversed my diabetes, and lowered my blood pressure and cholesterol to acceptable levels. Now, everyone deserves a chance to take their healing into their own hands, so I want to share my experience with the world.

Western or modern medicine doesn't have all the answers! With the information in this book, you can reverse damage to the digestive tract and gut, lower inflammation, and even combat autoimmune diseases by changing what and how you eat and learning to be mindful. However, those aren't all the benefits you'll get to enjoy. You'll also:

- Learn about different ways to heal yourself.
- Understand nutrition's role in the healing process.
- Discover how mindfulness can bring peace.
- Heal the gut to improve the inside and outside of yourself.

- Deal with inflammation.
- Boost your immune system.
- Learn how decades' worth of suffering can be overcome and relieved by making a few changes to your lifestyle.

Remember, a few modifications are worth it to feel relieved and be your old self again.

CHAPTER ONE

UNDERSTANDING THE MAJOR MEDICAL SYSTEMS

ALLOPATHY, AYURVEDIC, HOMEOPATHY, TRADITIONAL CHINESE MEDICINE (TCM), AND NATUROPATHY—AND THE LIMITATIONS OF WESTERN MEDICINE

> *Medicine is not only a science; it is also an art. It does not consist of compounding pills and plasters; it deals with the very processes of life, which must be understood before they may be guided*
>
> — PARACELSUS

Several types of medical systems are practiced and recognized throughout the world.

Allopathic medicine is also known as conventional, orthodox, main-stream, modern, or Western medicine. This is an evidence-based (science-backed) medicine that uses surgeries, therapies, and a variety of drugs approved by the Food and Drug Administration (FDA) (Sampson and Martin 2021).

Traditional Chinese medicine has been around for thousands of years, using psychological and physical approaches with herbal remedies. Traditional Chinese medicine is known to improve quality of life and fight against pain from many sources.

It includes treatments such as herbal remedies, acupuncture, and even tai chi:

- Acupuncture helps with chronic pain in the neck, lower back, knee, and even carpal tunnel syndrome. It also helps relieve tension, headaches, and migraines.
- Tai chi helps build physical strength and encourages mindfulness. It allows a person to improve their balance and stability, helps fight pain, and improves mood.
- Herbal remedies are used by one in five Americans (National Center for Complementary and Integrative Health [NCCIH], 2019b). However, these remedies aren't FDA approved or backed by science, even when there is much anecdotal evidence.

Ayurvedic is an ancient Indian medical practice used by almost a quarter of a million Americans (NCCIH, 2019a). Ayurvedic is considered the oldest medical practice in the world.

It relies on an integrated approach to helping with mental and physical health:

- Treatments are combinations of remedies (made with plant and animal parts with minerals and metals), lifestyle changes, exercise, diet, yoga, and pressure point treatment.
- Ayurvedic is known to help lower pain (especially in knees and rheumatoid arthritis), may assist in fighting against diabetes, and improve the quality of life.
- Herbal remedies aren't FDA approved; some treatments may contain toxic elements, such as lead.

Homeopathy was developed in Germany about two hundred years ago and is based on two theories:

- The first is that "like cures like." It's believed that an illness can be cured by using a substance that would cause its symptoms in a healthy person.
- The second is the "law of minimum dose." With this theory, it's believed that the lower the dose of the medication, the more effective it will be.

Homeopathy remedies are derived from plants, animals, or minerals and can come as creams, pills, tinctures, etc. In America, roughly five million adults and one million children use homeopathy remedies (NCCIH, 2021). Homeopathy is highly controversial and goes against the teachings of conventional medicine. The active ingredient in the medicine is what treats a symptom. With homeopathy medications being highly diluted, it isn't easy to scientifically test whether they'll be as effective as modern medication.

Naturopathy uses natural remedies to boost health and overall quality of life. When combined with other medical practices, naturopathy helps support the body's biological healing processes. Many different treatment approaches can range from detoxing to homeopathy, stress reduction, and even counseling. Most practitioners are recognized and accredited.

LIMITATIONS OF MEDICAL SYSTEMS

While all these practices are different, they have the same goals. They want to promote health and overall well-being. However, switching from one to the other isn't easy. It's important to discuss any traditional or alternative medicines you may want to try with your doctor before attempting them. There is a chance that natural remedies or modern medications can interact with each other.

Now that you better understand the available medical practices, it's time to consider why people keep returning to alternative medicines instead of using FDA-approved modern ones.

Chronic diseases are on the rise. The reasons for this vary from a poor diet (not getting adequate nutrition), a sedentary lifestyle (not getting enough exercise and movement), and exposure to various environmental toxins. Why is it that Western medicine is no longer able to cope with all these chronic diseases?

Western medicine isn't without its faults and limitations because it can't cure everything, no matter how great it is. Most Western medicines treat symptoms by targeting a specific body part instead of looking at the body as a whole. While they may well be called body parts, they are interconnected and not separate!

When a symptom or condition is treated, eventually, the symptom will disappear as the medicine targets it. Once the symptoms disappear, people believe they are cured, and the treatment is stopped. However, the symptom is destined to return, as the root cause of the problem was never discovered or treated. Ignoring the source of the problem will eventually lead to a chronic disease or recurrent symptoms.

Another limitation is modern medication's potential for side effects. Whenever you open a box of new medicine, a pamphlet details the potential side effects identified during the drug's testing phase. Some medicines are known for severe—and in some cases, deadly—side effects. The treatment of cancer is one such situation. Radiation and chemotherapy can do as much (if not more) harm to the body in hopes of treating the cancer by damaging healthy cells.

Conventional medicine relies a lot on tests and technology to determine the patient's problem. While not wrong, the overreliance on technology can be pricey, and it's not without problems, such as false positives or false negatives in test results. It can also lead to undiagnosed symptoms, even if only minor.

Modern medicine has been a reactive practice. Symptoms are treated after something has gone wrong with the body. Remaining reactive could lead to something more serious being missed, with eventual disastrous consequences. It's better to be *proactive* instead of reactive when treating a disease, as that will help diminish future symptoms. Prevention is far better than cure.

Another problem with modern medicine and chronic disease is the duration sufferers spend with the disorder. During this time, they could be seeing multiple practitioners, some of whom don't or won't read their medical files to see which treatments they have previously received. This leads to gaps in care, which can cause limitations or redundancies in their treatments—especially if some treatments have already been tried and failed—and add unnecessary costs. This sort of care can result in adverse patient outcomes, comorbidities, and even increased mortality rates.

Yes, allopathic medications have their shortcomings, but they have made remarkable strides in the health of billions of people worldwide, saving many who would likely not have survived without them. Most people use this medical practice, but it doesn't have to be the only one you use.

THE OVERRELIANCE ON PRESCRIPTION DRUGS

We have become too dependent on quick-fix prescriptions or even over-the-counter medications for common or minor medical disorders that inconvenience us. We often reach out for aspirin for headaches or statins to manage high cholesterol levels. Why? Because these are far easier solutions than changing a sedentary lifestyle, quitting smoking, and eating healthier. Lifestyle changes will decrease cholesterol levels, blood pressure, and other risk factors. The easy availability of these quick-fixing prescribed or over the counter and readily available medicines makes it easy for them to be abused or misused. There are more health benefits to changing a lifestyle, but most people are more likely to reach for the pills as they are more convenient.

One of the leading roles in the increased use of various medications is that pharmaceutical companies are allowed to advertise directly to the general public, not just doctors. While doctors have the medical knowledge to recognize if these medications can work well for a particular problem, the general population doesn't have the same knowledge. This results in someone with a particular problem coming to their doctor and requesting a specific type of medication for their condition.

Another problem is polypharmacy. When a person takes too many medications, this can lead to adverse effects from interactions between them. There's even a good chance that most of these medications aren't required in the first place. Polypharmacy is usually not intentional. A person can find themselves taking more medicines than needed by not understanding the instructions or being given a variety of medications to prevent side effects or allergic reactions. In the case of the elderly, a decline in cognitive function can also play a role in too many medications—or too much of one medication—being taken at a time. This is why people must know exactly what medications they're on and discuss their options with their healthcare provider to prevent them from being given similar medications that do the same function.

Yet, it isn't only patients who are responsible for polypharmacy. Inappropriate prescribing of medication from medical practitioners can be just as harmful. Medicines for chronic conditions aim to deal with potential future problems. This means a person could be taking medication for a potential problem for months, if not years, before lowering the risk of suffering from the problem, even if they aren't yet suffering from that problem.

This is also seen with antidepressants. Many doctors who prescribe antidepressants don't have the relevant training in mental health disorders and shouldn't be giving out this medication. That said, going to therapy to deal with the root of depression is expensive—especially with health insurance that doesn't reimburse the cost. Getting and giving pills is far easier. This is not to say there aren't people who benefit from taking pills, but as a society, we are becoming over-reliant on medication.

Dangers of Overreliance

There are many dangers surrounding overreliance on medications. Some can affect you personally, while others can affect other people.

Addiction and Overdose

- People on long-term pain medications can become addicted to them.
- Once addicted, it's easier to overdose as the medications are taken at higher than prescribed levels.

Adverse Effects

- Most medications come with warnings, side effects, and interactions. When taking multiple medications, there is a higher chance of these adverse effects occurring.
- Poor interactions with medications occur when patients aren't truthful (or are forgetful) about what they are taking or when multiple doctors working on the same patient aren't communicating.
- Many adverse effects are only noticed with long-term use.

Effect on Mental Health

- The excess or incorrect use of drugs aimed at mental health conditions (e.g., depression or anxiety) can lead to them becoming less effective over time.
- Some prescription drugs can cause the development of new mental health problems, while others (when used long-term) may contribute to cognitive function decline.

Antibiotic Resistance

- Unnecessary or incorrect use of prescribed antibiotics makes bacteria resistant over time due to their mutability.

- Bacteria have developed various resistance levels to all the antibiotics discovered in the last 70 years.
- This is why antibiotic courses should be completed and only used when prescribed.

Interactions

- Certain types of medications should never be taken at the same time, as they interact poorly with each other.
- While doctors know which medicines shouldn't be taken in conjunction, most people don't. This can lead to combinations of medications being taken that could result in serious health issues.
- This is why it's vital to know what medication you're on and be able to communicate this with your health practitioner.

Financial Burden

- Prescriptions are expensive, and their cost is increasing yearly. This cost will be even higher when out of pocket or when insurance insists on co-payments.
- The more medications you're on, the more it will cost.

LIMITATIONS OF WESTERN MEDICINE

As discussed earlier, there are limitations to Western medicine. Its approach to treatment is usually systemic, and the symptoms are used to determine what is wrong.

Before a person is diagnosed and treated, medical practitioners must physically examine and consider the symptoms. Science and experience are used to diagnose possible conditions and diseases. Once this occurs, clinically proven treatments help with the symptoms. This means only the noticed symptoms are treated, while the underlying condition (and even latent symptoms) go untreated.

Western medicine is great and has been developing for centuries. However, it's limited by its scientific approach to dealing with medical problems. Sometimes, the required treatments can cause unwanted side effects, causing almost as many issues as they fix. Consider Western medicine one of the tools to help you improve your health.

Antibiotics are given too readily, considering the damage they do to the body. Antibiotics are known to kill off bacteria; unfortunately, they do this indiscriminately, killing both good *and* bad varieties. Destroying populations of good bacteria can result in problems ranging from gut to skin issues.

As Western medicine's primary focus is evaluating symptoms and reacting to them, the reason for the symptoms is rarely explored, leaving the underlying problem undiscovered.

Long-term use of medication can cause chronic diseases to be suppressed and not dealt with for years. This could potentially result in severe side effects that can lead to life-threatening situations.

In time, chronic symptoms get worse, resulting in stronger medications being given to keep suppressing them. This can lead to addiction and overdose. There is even a chance of organ failure over time, resulting in death.

Doctors are rushed for time. They are given a set duration of time to spend with each patient. This limits doctors' patient interaction and the opportunity to ask in-depth questions. There is never enough time to glean all the information needed for an accurate diagnosis, and there is a chance something crucial can be missed. Even a minute mistake can cause a misdiagnosis, with incorrect medications being given, resulting in side effects or worse.

There are always pros and cons to using any medication. Allopathic medicine aims for the ill person to make a speedy recovery by curing the symptoms, yet it overlooks the possible causes.

It is worth remembering that allopathic medication has its place. It does wonders for traumatic injuries, but sometimes practitioners tend to become hyper-focused on the physical body, ignoring and neglecting the spiritual, emotional, and mental aspects, which could result in many different symptoms.

Allopathic medicine isn't the be-all and end-all of medicinal practices. You can benefit significantly from trying holistic approaches. However, don't trade one type of treatment for another. These are all tools to improve your life. Consider adding some holistic treatments as integrative medicines, and you'll be amazed by the changes in your health and wellness.

Many different medical systems are used around the world. While Western medicine is the most commonly used, some have started using holistic medicine to help alleviate their day-to-day problems. While many feel the need to rely on medicine from all medical practices heavily, this isn't the only way to deal with a chronic problem. The next chapter will explore using nutrition to support and self-heal your body.

CHAPTER TWO

WHAT WE CAN DO

SUPPORTING AND SELF-HEALING BY USING FOOD, NUTRITION, SUPPLEMENTS, HERBS, AND SPICES AS MEDICINE

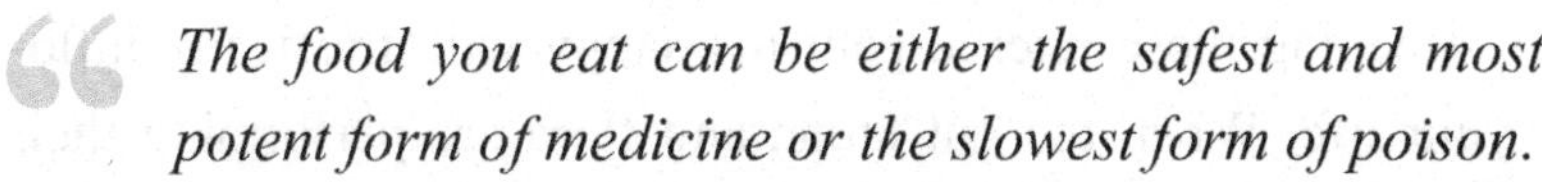

The food you eat can be either the safest and most potent form of medicine or the slowest form of poison.

— ANN WIGMORE

WHY FOOD AND NUTRITION MATTER

"You are what you eat" is a saying you have likely heard. In 1825, Anthelme Brillat-Savarin, a French politician and influential commentator on food, published *Physiologie du goût: Méditations de Gastronomie Transcendante*. This was later translated into English as the *Physiology of Taste or Meditations on Transcendental Gastronomy*. From this, we get the quote, "Tell me what you eat, and I shall tell you who you are."

We have known for centuries that food has an impact on our lives. This was ancient knowledge put forward by Greek and Roman physicians. However, our current understanding of modern nutrition occurred in the late 18th century; since then, science has been used to explain why we need food.

Food is made up of fats, proteins, carbohydrates, vitamins, and trace minerals—and it's used to fuel the body. Food isn't just fuel for the physical body; it powers our whole being emotionally and mentally. Food has a significant relationship with our feelings and moods. Sugary foods make many people happy, while spicy foods may result in a higher level of perceived aggressive behavior (Piedmont). Yet why does it affect us?

Food affects your gastrointestinal tract. The brain and gut are connected through the brain-gut axis, so the gastrointestinal tract is also known as our second brain. This digestive tract contains billions of microorganisms, including bacteria, fungi, viruses, and yeasts. Keeping these microorganisms happy will drastically influence your life. When the gut fauna and flora are performing their various functions in the gut, they affect the production of neurotransmitters, the chemicals used to send messages around the body. The gut also has more serotonin receptors, making people happier, especially after eating. Eating a well-balanced diet results in a healthier life and drastically influences our mood.

However, gut health can be significantly altered with a poor diet high in processed food and antibiotics. The good bacteria will be negatively influenced, allowing pathogens to take over and cause problems. This causes you to feel ill and leads to issues such as fibromyalgia. Eating poorly will always make you feel terrible, but when you eat well, you get a good sleep, have lots of energy, a better mood, and an improved digestive system. So, don't expect to feel good if you're filling up on poor-quality foods.

It isn't just gut health that's affected by what you eat. Food can alter our very DNA. To help create these building blocks of life, organisms need to eat and drink; therefore, the composition of their genes will be directly influenced by what is consumed. Every day, cells in the body are being destroyed and replaced, and to do this, food is used as a source of energy.

Oxford's Department of Plant Sciences hypothesizes that food composition can alter an organism's DNA due to the strong relationship between cellular metabolism and evolution (Pastor Guzman, 2020). This has led scientists to believe that DNA sequences can be influenced by an organism adapting to different foods due to availability or dietary changes. Because of this, scientists have developed the theory that a diet can be accurately predicted just by looking at an organism's DNA sequence.

Understanding Nutrition

When it comes to food, making wise choices is a must. Food is fuel; it keeps you healthy and decreases the risk factors for many chronic diseases. Navigating good nutrition can be difficult, and often, you will hear the terms *good* or *bad* food. There is no good or bad food, but relatively *nutritious* or *non-nutritious* foods. However, you don't have to be a dietitian to learn which foods are better for you.

Your daily tasks require the necessary energy to complete them and the nutrients to help keep you going. These are used throughout the day and need replenishing. This means eating well-balanced meals—containing vitamins, minerals, proteins, fats, and carbohydrates—and drinking a suitable volume of water daily. How much you require of each will depend on your age, gender, activity level, and even where you live. For those over 50, some vitamins and minerals may be required.

A highly nutritious diet should be rich in natural foods. This includes vegetables and fruits in as many colors as possible for the antioxidant effects, whole grains for fiber and better digestion, dairy products (preferably low-fat and being wary of those that come sweetened), and protein in the form of lean meats, poultry, fish, eggs, soy products, legumes, and nuts.

Food types you want to keep to a minimum or avoid altogether include highly processed foods, which are high in sodium and contribute to high blood pressure; foods high in cholesterol; foods that are fried and high in trans fats; refined carbohydrates (e.g., white sugar or white flour); and alcohol.

The healthier the diet, the longer life you'll enjoy and the lower the chance of developing chronic diseases, as their risks are diminished. It's never too late to adopt a healthy diet, as even if you already suffer from a chronic disease, a more nutritious diet will help manage the condition while avoiding complications.

A healthy diet takes a lot of work and isn't possible for everyone. Sadly, unhealthy options tend to be cheaper, leading people to consume foods high in sodium, saturated fats, and sugar.

Poor diets and some conditions—such as losing parts of the intestines—result in not getting the necessary nutrition required for the body to function the way it should. This can lead to a range of deficiencies that can cause poor health and debilitating conditions. Diseases such as scurvy (lack of vitamin C) and anemia (low iron levels) are some of the most well-known deficiencies that can occur. In some cases, a lack of vitamins, such as vitamin D, can cause the body not to absorb other vital nutrients; in this case, failure to adequately absorb calcium can lead to a loss in bone density.

While poor diets can lead to the deficiencies that cause diseases, they can also increase the risk factors for chronic diseases. Consuming too many calories, especially empty calories, increases weight, leading to obesity. Contributing factors to heart disease and strokes include high sodium, high cholesterol, and high blood pressure. Type 2 diabetes can develop over time due to increased weight, obesity, and consuming too much sugar; this causes insulin resistance and prediabetes. There are even 13 different cancers caused by poor nutrition, including—but not limited to—breast, colon, and uterus cancers. Diets high in salt—commonly seen in the modern diet—but low in vegetables and whole grains can lead to hypertension (high blood pressure), heart disease, stroke, and type 2 diabetes. Avoiding a poor diet is easy when you have the necessary knowledge; here are some handy hints:

Be careful with salt.

- There are a variety of salts that can be consumed. Generally, you'll be ingesting sodium and potassium when eating salt.
- The body needs both of these, but an imbalance of the two can cause many problems to certain organs—brain, kidneys, heart, and eyes—and increase blood pressure, which is bad for people with existing kidney issues.
- The imbalance is at its worst with a diet high in sodium and low in potassium.

Beware of dietary trends.

- There are always new fad diets that make promises they can't keep and can cause more problems than they fix.

- Modifying most diets is as easy as lowering salt intake, refraining from empty calories, eating more vegetables, and being mindful of the fats and proteins you consume.

Drink enough water.

- Hydration plays a vital role in all metabolic processes in the body.
- How much water is required depends on many factors, but it has been suggested that men drink up to 13 cups, while women should have up to 9 (Harvard School of Public Health, 2019).
- While pure water is great for any diet, some people can't stomach the taste. Water infusions should be considered to prevent sweetened syrups from being added to change the taste. Add some of your favorite fruits and herbs to your water and allow the flavor to be absorbed before drinking it.

Try plant-based meals.

- Trading an animal-based meal for a plant-based one will do wonders for your health.
- This switch will encourage the consumption of healthy fats, fibers, and more fruits and vegetables.
- However, be careful of falling for all foods labeled as vegan or vegetarian because, while plant-based, they may not necessarily be healthy. Oreos are considered vegan, and they are high in sugar.
- Plant-based meals are known to help those suffering from chronic kidney disease (CKD).

Watch the sugar content.

- Sugar is a carbohydrate that the body needs but should be limited.
- When consuming large quantities of sugar, lots of glucose is released into the bloodstream. To compensate for this, the pancreas secretes insulin in lower concentrations. Eventually, the excess insulin will cause insulin resistance, and the body will no longer react to insulin similarly.
- If the diet isn't changed, there is a chance that type 2 diabetes will develop.
- People tend to ingest too much sugar because pre-made meals are generally higher in added sugars, or they consume sweetened drinks.

Water isn't the only liquid you can drink.

- Coffee and tea—when drunk without the addition of sugar, sweetened syrups, or creams—are fine in moderation. Tea has many benefits, such as lowering the risk of stroke, heart disease, and even type 2 diabetes.
- High alcohol consumption can cause an increase in heart disease and blood pressure. Extended abuse of alcohol can be deadly to the brain and liver while increasing the risk of strokes and even mental health problems. Alcohol is also a diuretic and will increase water loss, leading to dehydration and kidney damage in the long run.
- Sodas and fruit juices tend to be full of excess sugar and are best avoided, as regular use can increase the risk of obesity; type 2 diabetes; diseases of the liver, heart, and kidney; and dental issues. Fruit juices, while full of benefits, don't have the fiber content to prevent the spike of

glucose that comes with the high sugar content. Consume sparingly or watered down.

Even with all these handy tips, it can be challenging to make the correct choices when it comes to diet. Remember, there is no need to make changes immediately. Start slowly and get your body prepared for the adjustments. Take the time to list foods high in vitamins, fiber, and minerals. A diet with a wide range of foods will give you all the necessary nutrients. Take the time to select nutrient-dense foods, ensuring high levels of fiber, vitamins, and minerals.

Vitamins

Vitamins can be divided into groups: those that are water soluble and those that are fat soluble. The water-soluble vitamins are C and B complex: B1–B3, B5–B7, B9, and B12; when in excess, they will be excreted, usually through the urine. The fat-soluble vitamins are A, D, E, and K; these are stored in the liver and fatty tissues when in excess. In the table below are some examples of foods that contain different types of vitamins.

Water-Soluble Vitamins:

- Vitamin B1 (Thiamin) is found in fish, pork, beans, lentils, sunflower seeds, and green peas.
- B2 (Riboflavin) is found in dairy products such as milk, yogurt, and cheese; eggs; beef liver; almonds; lean beef; salmon; pork; spinach; and enriched grains.
- Vitamin B3 (Niacin) is found in red meat, poultry, seeds, brown rice, bananas, nuts, and lentils.
- B5 (Pantothenic acid) is found in beef; organ meats; poultry; seafood; eggs; milk; vegetables such as

mushrooms, potatoes, and broccoli; whole grains, especially whole wheat, brown rice, and oats; peanuts; chickpeas; sunflower seeds; and avocados.

- Vitamin B6 (Pyridoxine) is found in beef liver, poultry, tuna, salmon, fortified cereals, chickpeas, and various vegetables and fruits—including dark leafy greens, cantaloupe, oranges, bananas, and papayas.
- B7 (Biotin) is found in beef liver, eggs, salmon, pork, avocados, sweet potatoes, nuts, and seeds.
- Vitamin B9 (also known as folate or folic acid) is found in dark green leafy vegetables such as romaine lettuce, turnip greens, asparagus, spinach, broccoli, and Brussel sprouts; beans; peanuts; fruits; whole grains; eggs; seafood; liver; and sunflower seeds.
- B12 (Cobalamin) is found in fish, shellfish, liver, poultry, red meat, eggs, and dairy products.
- Vitamin C (Ascorbic acid) is found in citrus fruits like oranges, grapefruit, and lemon; other fruits such as kiwi, bell peppers, strawberries, and tomatoes; and cruciferous vegetables like cauliflower, broccoli, cabbage, Brussels sprouts, and white potatoes.

Fat-Soluble Vitamins:

- Vitamin A (Retinol) is found in leafy green vegetables like kale, spinach, and broccoli; orange and yellow vegetables such as sweet potato, carrots, and all squashes; tomatoes; red bell pepper; cantaloupe; mango; milk; eggs; beef liver; and fish oils.
- Vitamin D (Calciferol) is found in cod liver oil; fish like salmon, swordfish, sardines, and tuna; fortified drinks such as orange juice, dairy, and plant milks; beef liver; and egg

yolk.

- Vitamin E (Tocopherol) is found in a variety of oils such as wheat germ, sunflower, safflower, and soybean; nuts and seeds, especially sunflower seeds and almonds; peanuts and peanut butter; vegetables including asparagus, beet greens, collard greens, pumpkin, spinach, and red bell pepper; as well as mangoes and avocados.
- Vitamin K includes K1 (Phylloquinone) and K2 (Menaquinones).
    - Vitamin K1 is found in green leafy vegetables like spinach, collard and turnip greens, broccoli, kale, cabbage, Brussels sprouts, and various lettuces; oils including soybean and canola (as well as salad dressings made with soybean or canola oil); and fortified meals.
    - Vitamin K2 is found in natto or fermented soybeans, meat, cheese, and eggs.

Almost everything you eat will contain vitamins. The more varied your diet, especially if it is filled with colors, the more vitamins you consume.

Minerals

The body requires both major and trace minerals to function correctly. The only difference is how much the body needs of each.

Major minerals include:

- **Calcium:** found in dairy, fortified plant-based milk, fortified orange juice, winter squash, almonds, leafy greens, edamame or young green soybeans, tofu with calcium sulfate, and canned sardines or salmon with bones.

- **Chloride:** found in table, sea, and kosher salt; seaweed; shrimp; processed foods; and condiments high in sodium such as deli meats, cheese, potato chips, hot dogs, ketchup, soy sauce, and Worcestershire sauce.
- **Magnesium:** found in almonds, pumpkin seeds, cashews, peanuts, peanut butter, beans, soybeans, soymilk, leafy greens, white potato with skin, grains such as brown rice and oatmeal, salmon, beef, poultry, banana, raisins, dark chocolate with at least 70% pure cocoa, and dairy like milk and yogurt.
- **Potassium:** found in dried fruits like raisins and apricots; vegetables such as potatoes, winter squash, spinach, tomatoes, broccoli, and beet greens; beans; lentils; fruits like avocado, bananas, cantaloupe, and oranges; coconut water; dairy like milk and yogurt; plant milks; cashews; almonds; chicken; and salmon.
- **Sodium:** found in vegetables and table salt.

Minor minerals include:

- **Chromium:** found in whole grains including high-fiber bran cereals; vegetables like broccoli, green beans, and potatoes; apples; bananas; beef; poultry; fish; eggs; coffee; brewer's yeast; and certain brands of beer and red wine.
- **Copper:** found in beef liver, oysters, crab, salmon, unsweetened dark chocolate, cashews, sunflower, sesame seeds, chickpeas, millet, whole-wheat pasta, potatoes, and spinach.

- **Fluoride:** found in brewed black tea and coffee, fluoridated water, canned shellfish like shrimp and blue crab, oatmeal, raisins, and potatoes.
- **Iodine:** found in seaweed such as nori, kombu, kelp, and wakame; fish, shellfish like cod, canned tuna, oysters, and shrimp; iodized table salt, dairy, eggs, beef liver, and chicken.
- **Iron:** found in oysters, clams, mussels, organ meats, canned sardines or tuna, beef, poultry, beans, dark chocolate, lentils, spinach, potato with skin, nuts, seeds, and enriched grains.
- **Manganese:** found in almonds, cashews, pumpkin seeds, peanuts, soybeans, soymilk, peanut butter, beans, spinach, Swiss chard, white potato with skin, grains like oatmeal and brown rice, dark chocolate, raisins, milk, yogurt, salmon, beef, poultry, and banana.
- **Selenium:** found in walnuts, Brazil nuts, fish, shellfish, beef, turkey, chicken, fortified cereals, whole-wheat bread, beans, and lentils.
- **Zinc:** found in shellfish, beef, poultry, pork, legumes, nuts, seeds, and whole grains.

As with vitamins, the more varied your diet, the more varied your mineral intake will be.

Fiber

r helps keep your bowel movements regular, lowers
owers the risk of colorectal cancer and heart disease,
sugar spikes, and keeps you fuller for longer,
ght loss due to consuming fewer calories. Due to
of fiber, it also acts as a prebiotic for your gut

microbiome—feeding them, which in turn comes with many benefits.

Fiber strictly comes from plant-based foods. You're getting fiber regardless of what fruits, vegetables, seeds, nuts, and whole grains you eat. Here are a few great examples to start adding to your diet:

- **Fruits:** raspberries, blackberries, pears, Hass variety avocados, and apples
- **Grains:** whole-wheat pasta, barley, rolled or steel-cut oats, and quinoa
- **Legumes:** lentils; split and green peas; pinto, black, and kidney beans; chickpeas, and edamame
- **Nuts and seeds:** chia seeds, almonds, and ground flaxseed.
- **Vegetables:** artichoke hearts, broccoli, and Brussels sprouts

If you struggle to get fiber into your diet, look at ways to incorporate it with snacks such as air-popped popcorn with nothing added, bananas with nuts, carrots and hummus, and celery and peanut butter.

Low fiber levels result in constipation, as well as an increased risk of heart disease, colon cancer, and type 2 diabetes. Adding extra fiber slowly to your diet is essential, as adding too much can result in bloating and other gastrointestinal issues. Drinking more water will help protect against constipation.

Don't feel limited to these foods to get the necessary fiber, minerals, and vitamins for your diet. Adding herbs and spices can also contribute to your health if you use them correctly! These plant-based goods are generally high in antioxidants, which is excellent for dealing with daily oxidative stresses. Herbs and spices are also a great way to reduce salt usage! Herbs and spices aren't just for cooking and baking; each herb and spice contain various compounds with properties ranging from anti-inflammatory to cancer-fighting and can even help lower cholesterol.

THE SELF-HEALING POWER OF THE HUMAN BODY

The human body is an amazing self-healing machine. It can heal from the tiniest scratch to a broken bone, which is good, as accumulated wounds and illnesses would have wiped out humans long ago if it couldn't. It's something we don't have to think about; it's built into our very DNA, and even though medication is often prescribed, it's aimed at helping the body heal f5aster. Some injuries and illnesses are quickly overcome, while others take some time. However, there is a chance that an injury or disease takes longer than it should to heal or that it's a recurring problem. It will continue to be a recurring problem until the cause of the problem is discovered and dealt with. A healthy body can heal, fight infections, repair damage, and fight back against the first signs of aging.

Many factors can influence how quickly, or even *if*, a body can self-heal. Most problems occur when the immune system is suppressed in some manner. This can be caused by not getting enough sleep—as the body does most of its healing while you sleep. Other contributing factors include age, weight, not getting enough exercise, high levels of stress, toxins, a poor diet, and having a poor mindset.

The first sign that something is wrong with your body is a fever, showing the body has an infection or inflammation—which is a reaction to an infection or injury. The body's health can also be disrupted by oxidative stress caused by free radicals and disease. By getting the necessary rest and exercise, the body can put up a good fight against almost anything. However, this requires a lot of energy, and the only way to get that is through eating. When eating a diet rich in nutrients, the body is fueled with the necessary minerals, vitamins, and energy to help it self-heal.

A poor diet lacking the necessary nutrients will result in inflammation and digestive issues and leave the body unable to self-heal. This means illnesses and injuries take much longer to heal, causing the immune system to endure a lot of strain and, over an extended period, lead to chronic inflammation, especially in the gut. This will birth a myriad of chronic diseases.

Even if you're already suffering from chronic inflammation, changing your diet to healthier foods will help the healing process. It's never too late to make the necessary alterations and lower the chance of your chronic issues worsening.

GOOD AND NUTRITIOUS FOODS TO EAT

It's easy to tell someone to eat healthier, but it's considerably more challenging to know how to. Many foods are labeled as healthy, but when you look at the contents, you're met with a variety of ingredients that may cause inflammation in your body. Ideally, when it comes to healthy food, you want to avoid prepackaged and processed meals. The best foods to consume are those that haven't been refined too much. Here are some of the best foods to include in your diet:

Nuts

Almonds are high in fiber, calcium, magnesium, iron, vitamin E, and B2. They help lower cholesterol and protect against diminished vision and cataract development.

Brazil nuts are high in vitamins B1 and E and magnesium, zinc, and selenium minerals. They are good for the thyroid.

Grains

Oatmeal is high in fiber, folate, and potassium. It helps lower cholesterol, and due to being a complex carbohydrate, its slow digestion prevents excessive spikes in blood glucose.

Quinoa is high in fiber and protein. It has a low glycemic index, allowing for fewer glucose spikes.

Wheat germs are often removed from grains during the refining process due to their high fat content, which affects the stability of the product. It's high in fiber, vitamin E, folic acid, essential fatty acids, fatty alcohols, B1, phosphorus, magnesium, and zinc.

Vegetables

Broccoli and other cruciferous vegetables contain a sulforaphane compound with anticancer and anti-inflammatory properties. Broccoli also contains the compound glucosinolates that help detoxify the body. It's high in fiber, calcium, phytonutrients, folates, vitamin C, and beta-carotene. Phytonutrients help to lower the risk of some cancers, heart disease, and diabetes.

Regardless of color, beets are high in carotenoids that help with improvement in endurance training. Beets also help lower inflammation, boost growth and development, help with eye health, and increase the immune system.

Kale is high in vitamin C, fiber, and antioxidants. It is nutrient-dense and helps lower cholesterol.

Leafy green vegetables are high in lutein and zeaxanthin, which helps lower the risk of vision degeneration. They're also high in antioxidants; vitamins A, B6, C, E, and K; iron; selenium; zinc; manganese; calcium; copper; and potassium.

Sweet potatoes are high in fiber; vitamins A, B6, and C; potassium; and calcium. They are complex carbohydrates that take a while to digest and release sugar slowly into the blood.

Pickled vegetables are a great source of probiotics, minerals, and vitamins—depending on the vegetable used.

Fruits

Apples are high in antioxidants and fiber. Red apples are delicious as they contain the anti-inflammatory flavonoid quercetin found in red fruits and vegetables.

Avocados are high in healthy fats such as high-density lipoprotein and help eliminate poor cholesterol. They can also help with absorbing nutrients.

Blueberries are high in fiber, antioxidants, and phytonutrients. They help protect the brain against cognitive decline by reducing the risk of dementia and Alzheimer's disease, lowering blood pressure, and maybe even helping to prevent heart disease.

Mangoes are high in fiber, minerals, and vitamins A and C.

Protein

Oily fish are high in omega-3 fatty acids—which help fight inflammation—and vitamins A and D. They help lower the chance of stroke, cancer, and heart disease. Oily fish include salmon, anchovies, mackerel, sardines, and herrings.

Chicken is high in protein, low in fat, and generally affordable meat.

Eggs are high in protein with many ways to prepare them. They contain vitamins B2 and B12 that help with energy and red blood cell production. Eggs have two essential amino acids: leucine helps make muscles, and choline makes cell membranes. Eggs contain good fats but should be eaten in moderation.

Healthy Fats

Olive oil, ideally extra-virgin olive oil, is high in anti-inflammatory properties.

Pulses and Legumes

Lentils are high in fiber, protein, magnesium, and potassium. They can be enjoyed as sprouts, microgreens, or dried.

Peanut butter is high in proteins, carbohydrates, and good fats. Choose a variety that is low in sugar and salt. Peanut butter has a low glycemic index, allowing for fewer glucose spikes in the blood.

To get all the benefits from fruits and vegetables, ensure they are eaten raw or lightly steamed to prevent water-soluble vitamins being damaged.

When choosing grains, opt to eat as many whole grains as possible, such as whole wheat, rye, oatmeal, barley, amaranth, quinoa, or multi-grains, to name a few! All grains start as whole grains, but they get refined to produce foods such as white rice or white flour.

Grain comprises three parts: the endosperm (the white part), the germ, and the bran. The bran and germ are stripped away when refined, leaving only the endosperm. While this part of the grain has some benefits, the main benefits have been stripped away.

The germ is high in good fats, while the bran contains fiber, vitamins B5 and E, minerals (e.g., copper, magnesium, and selenium), nutrients, phytochemicals, and more healthy fats. The bran also helps to maintain blood sugar and prevent glucose spikes after eating. The high fiber content helps to lower cholesterol and increases the removal of waste from the digestive tract. Whole grains may even help reduce heart attacks and strokes by preventing the formation of blood clots. The phytochemicals in whole grains are protective against some cancers.

Including whole grains in your diet is a sure way to fight back against inflammation, heart disease, and type 2 diabetes while improving digestive health. However, it's not just about what you eat—it's about variety, balance, and quantity. A variety of the foods above—together with more fruits and vegetables—will ensure you get all your nutrients and as many vitamins and minerals as needed by your body.

Variety is good, but it also needs to be balanced. Eating various healthy foods is great but be mindful of the number of calories you consume. Eating more calories than you burn will increase weight, regardless of how healthy your diet is—which brings us to moderation.

Moderation isn't just about keeping your calories within an acceptable range; it's also about limiting certain foods. Controlling how much of something you eat is important, especially when it comes to foods considered unhealthy. Chocolate—especially dark chocolate—is great for your health when enjoyed in moderation. The

Mediterranean diet—often held up as the best—allows for moderate consumption of alcohol. Chocolate and alcohol are considered unhealthy by many but shouldn't be when enjoyed in moderation.

FOODS TO AVOID

A diet of poor fats, too much sugar, and processed foods will eventually lead to chronic inflammation. However, it can be difficult to make sudden dietary changes. Instead of scrapping your diet, add more fruits and vegetables while slowly cutting out the following foods or additions.

Added Sugar

Beware of products that state, "added sugar" or "sweetened," as extra sugar has been added. This can include more white or brown sugar, high-fructose sugar, corn syrup, and numerous other types of sugar.

These sugars are pure carbohydrates that aren't buffered by fiber. Consuming foods with added sugar will cause glucose spikes in the blood that insulin may struggle to control.

Sweetened drinks have a lot of calories, but they are considered empty, as they don't fill your stomach. This results in you still feeling hungry despite consuming so many calories.

Baked goods have high levels of added sugar. However, they are also high in refined grains, known as white carbs.

Processed Meats

Processed meats have a long ingredient list, making them a poor substitute for healthy, lean proteins. These are generally high in poor fats and salt.

Refined Foods

Refined foods have the fiber removed. The food is easier to chew and digest with no fiber but can lead to constipation and a poor gut microbiome.

Refined Seed Oils

These types of oils are high in linoleic acid, which is known to cause health issues. Consuming high amounts of these oils could result in obesity, heart disease, cancer, and diabetes. They are high in omega-6 fatty acids. They cause inflammation and oxidative stress, and when uncontrolled, can even lead to autoimmune diseases and Alzheimer's.

Junk Food

Although great for a once-in-a-while treat, it sadly has become a staple due to its convenience. It's high in saturated and trans fats, sugars, and salt. This contributes to increased weight, which leads to obesity and metabolic disease that can further develop into type 2 diabetes.

Salt

Too much sodium can cause high blood pressure that can lead to chronic issues developing in the heart, eyes, brain, and kidneys, eventually leading to heart attacks and strokes.

Saturated Fats

You want to avoid consuming a lot of saturated fats, as it can lead to obesity and high cholesterol, leading to other chronic diseases. Avoid fried and excessively fatty foods.

Another helpful hint is to simply eat less food. When you're eating nutrient-dense foods, you don't require as much, meaning you can get away with smaller portions.

Tips for Healthy Eating

Healthy eating isn't as difficult as most people think:

- Breakfast is important, so make it count with a well-balanced meal full of complex carbohydrates, healthy fats, and protein. Breakfast helps jumpstart the metabolism and get the brain working.
- Calories aren't the only factors you should count on in your diet. Know how to read a nutritional label.
- Consume enough calories throughout the day and avoid restricting calories too much.
- Enjoy what you eat. It's more than just fueling your body; it's about building a better future with your body.

- Ensure that half your plate is filled with vegetables, preferably of the dark green variety. The next quarter should be filled with legumes or whole grains.
- Expand your palate with different whole grains. They're healthier and contain all the fiber you need. Learn to distinguish complex carbohydrates from simple ones.
- Know what goes into food preparation when you're eating out. Make healthy choices and ask to have your salad dressings and sauces on the side.
- Limit your processed food consumption. It may be convenient, but in the long run, it can be dangerous with its hidden fats, sugars, and salts.
- Never go shopping without a list and a cooking plan. Doing this allows you to only buy what you need and avoid buying prepackaged goods.
- Watch your sugar and salt intake, especially when eating prepackaged goods.

Start your dietary changes slowly by eliminating your processed junk food and snacks. There are many recipes and ideas online for healthier snack options.

ARE SUPPLEMENTS REQUIRED?

Supplements can be beneficial depending on what you're supplementing. However, they shouldn't be considered a quick fix to a dietary problem. Most aren't FDA approved, so it can be challenging to determine the possible side effects. When using supplements, be aware of potential side effects and interactions with various medications.

In the case of a healthy and well-balanced diet, supplements are usually not required, as nutrient-dense food should provide everything you need. There are exceptions to this. Some people may need to take supplements because they can't absorb enough nutrients from their diet, such as those who have shortened bowels. Other reasons include:

- People with dietary restrictions that prevent them from getting the required nutrients.
- Anyone over 50 will need increased vitamins B12 and D and calcium. Vitamin D and calcium are crucial to prevent osteoporosis and weaken bones. Vitamin B12 becomes more difficult to absorb with age, so more is required.
- Soil depletion due to extensive farming causes some foods to lack certain nutrients. Eating those foods won't be enough, so supplements will be needed.
- Other people want a backup to their diet—a vitamin insurance policy—which will help manage any deficiencies.
- Supplements are great for boosting the health of people considered at risk (e.g., those who are pregnant, ill, or diabetic).

The most common supplements include vitamins B2, B6, C, and E, as well as the *minerals* zinc, magnesium, calcium, phosphorus, and iron. Generally, it's best to have a doctor tell you which supplements you need to improve your life. Taking supplements isn't an excuse for a poor diet. It's a supplement meant to enhance your diet, not a replacement. While extra vitamins and minerals are meant to be helpful, consuming too many of those with an upper limit will cause toxicities that are detrimental to your health. They can also interact with medicines, whether alternative or traditional.

Supplements aren't regulated as stringently as pharmaceutical medicine, so be wary when purchasing. Carefully read the label to see what ingredients are used and what is being supplemented. Be sure to talk to your doctor before taking supplements to avoid possible negative interactions.

SUPPLEMENTS FOR CHRONIC DISEASES AND PAIN

Some supplements can be used to help fight chronic diseases and pain. However, they need to be coupled with a healthy lifestyle and a well-balanced diet to lower the chance of inflammation. The supplements that can be used are vitamins, minerals, botanicals such as herbs and spices, and digestive enzymes.

Choosing the right supplements can be difficult as some products claim they can cure or prevent diseases. These false promises are illegal. Don't be fooled by them. When choosing a supplement, there are a few things you need to look over carefully. The first is the supplement fact label, similar to a nutritional label. This label will tell you what is in the supplement, including other mixed ingredients such as filler or flavorings.

The recommended daily allowance (RDA) and the daily value (DV) would be best. These two factors aren't the same. The RDA is the allowance of vitamins and minerals for a healthy person and lets you know what is recommended for a person depending on their age, gender, or if they're pregnant or breastfeeding. The DV is similar but is recommended for anyone over the age of four. Some numbers are well above 100%, but don't worry. These are generally for minerals and vitamins that don't have an upper limit, and you can have an excess of them since it's rare to suffer toxicity from consuming too much.

How much of a supplement you need can be challenging to figure out. This is why it's so important for you to speak to your healthcare provider, as they can assist you with this. They will also inform you about the benefits and risks of using dietary supplements. It's great to get a boost from supplements such as vitamin D, omega-3 fatty acids, and calcium, but it's better to get these through your diet, if possible.

Chronic pain is the leading cause of disability in adults in the United States, and many are treated using opiates. While opiates are great at what they do, they are highly addictive, causing more problems while not solving the underlying reason behind the pain. Some vitamins and minerals that help with chronic pain are vitamins A, C, and magnesium. However, there are many more that can help.

Vitamins

Without vitamins, the body couldn't function or fight back infections. Each vitamin has a specific job in the body.

- **Vitamin A (retinol)** is good for the eyes and offers some protection against cancers. It supports cellular growth and maintains the health of the heart, lungs, and eyes.
- **Vitamin B1 (thiamin)** is used to help make energy and facilitate the growth, development, and function of cells.
- **Vitamin B2 (riboflavin)** can convert amino acids and vitamins to perform various bodily functions. It helps maintain the amino acid homocysteine in the blood. This is required to make two coenzymes involved in energy production; increasing cellular growth, function, and development; and assisting with the metabolism of steroids, fats, and drugs.

- Without **vitamin B3 (niacin)**, hundreds of enzymes would cease functioning.
- **Vitamin B5 (pantothenic acid)** is required to make coenzyme A (CoA) used in the making and breaking down of fatty acids. The acyl carrier protein which plays a role in making fatty acids.
- **Vitamin B6 (pyridoxine)** is a highly versatile vitamin comprising six vitamers (compounds). It plays a role in gluconeogenesis, glycogenolysis, immune function, and cognitive development; it also helps produce hemoglobin. B6 helps maintain homocysteine in the blood. It assists in the metabolism of proteins, amino acids, carbohydrates, and fats.
- **Vitamin B7 (biotin)** is crucial for creating five carboxylases that metabolize fatty acids, glucose, and amino acids. It plays a role in cell signaling, gene regulation, and histone (a group of proteins) modifications.
- **Vitamin B9 (folate, formic acid)** aids in synthesizing nucleic acids (DNA and RNA) and plays a role in the metabolism of amino acids.
- **Vitamin B12 (cobalamin)** is required for the central nervous system to develop, get myelinated, and function correctly.
- The body cannot make **vitamin C (ascorbic acid)** and so must consume it. It's used to make some neurotransmitters, collagen, and L-carnitine—which is used to turn fat into energy. It assists in protein metabolism and wound healing. This vitamin helps limit the damage caused by free radicals. It protects against cancers (especially stomach cancer) and prevents scurvy. Vitamin C plays a role in immune function.

- **Vitamin D (calciferol)** allows calcium absorption in the gut while preventing muscle cramps and strengthening bones. It helps muscles and nerves communicate and is required for bone growth and repair. It lowers inflammation, helps with cellular growth and glucose metabolism, and boosts immune function.
- **Vitamin E (tocopherol)** is an antioxidant that lowers oxidative stress damage when fat is oxidized. It helps with immune function. This vitamin regulates gene expression, cell signaling, and other metabolic processes.
- **Vitamin K** includes both **phylloquinone** (K1) and **menaquinones** (K2). Vitamin K helps with blood clotting and bone metabolism.

Minerals

Different minerals have different jobs in the body, but generally, they are used to keep your bones strong while allowing your heart, brain, and muscles to function correctly. They are also vital in the production of enzymes and hormones.

- **Calcium** is required to maintain the body's structure by strengthening bones and teeth. This mineral facilitates body movement by allowing it to be flexible, rigid, or strong when needed. Other functions include helping with hormone secretion, contracting and dilating of blood vessels, nerve transmission, muscular function, and blood clotting.
- **Chloride** is an electrolyte that helps regulate the fluid levels of cells and the nutrients that travel through them. Chloride helps stimulate cells, nerves, and stomach acid

while maintaining its pH level. It allows for the movement of oxygen and carbon dioxide through cells.

- **Chromium** plays a possible role in the metabolism of proteins, carbohydrates, and fats by increasing the effectiveness of insulin.
- Many enzymes require **copper** to help generate energy, create connective tissue and neurotransmitters, metabolize iron, and activate neuropeptides (chemical messengers). It's also used to develop capillaries from larger blood vessels, for pigmentation (coloration), to regulate gene expression, for brain development, for homeostasis of neurohormones, and to support the immune system function. Copper is an antioxidant and protects against oxidative damage.
- **Fluoride** inhibits and reverses the start of tooth decay. It also triggers new bone formation.
- **Iodine** is required to make the thyroid hormones vital for creating proteins, enzymes, and metabolic activity. This mineral is necessary for developing the central nervous system and the skeletal structure during fetal development and in young babies.
- **Iron** is necessary for the hemoglobin to carry oxygen in the blood. Iron is required to help with muscle metabolism and create healthy connective tissue. It's also used to create some hormones and helps with physical growth, neurological development, and correct cellular function.
- **Magnesium** is used in various enzymes that assist with making protein, aid in muscle and nerve function, control blood sugar, and help regulate blood pressure. It's required to produce energy, develop bone, and create DNA and RNA. Magnesium is necessary to transport calcium and potassium over cell membranes, which is needed to help

contract muscles, aid nerve impulse conduction, and maintain a normal heart rhythm.

- **Manganese** is a cofactor of many enzymes that help make amino acids, cholesterol, carbohydrates, and glucose. It assists with bone formation, reproduction, and immune response. Together with vitamin K, this mineral helps with blood clotting.
- **Potassium** maintains the fluid levels within the cells, working together with sodium, which holds the fluid levels outside. Potassium helps keep blood pressure regular and aids in muscle contractions.
- **Selenium** is an antioxidant; it protects from oxidative stresses and infections. Selenium also plays a role in thyroid hormone metabolism, the creation of DNA, and reproduction.
- **Sodium** is required as an electrolyte but needs to be monitored, as it can lead to high blood pressure if too much is consumed.
- **Zinc** helps improve immune function, creates protein and DNA, boosts healing, and assists in cell signaling and cell division. This mineral is required for the healthy growth and development of fetuses during pregnancy and children until adolescence. Zinc is also involved in the sense of taste.

Remember that there is no substitution for a healthy, well-balanced diet. Supplementing vitamins and minerals should only be done to guard against deficiencies and when managing chronic disease and pain.

Knowing when to take certain supplements and how much to take can be daunting. If you want more information, use the online resource from the Office of Dieting Supplements: (https://ods.od.nih.gov/About/ODS_Videos.aspx)

Botanicals

Botanical dietary supplements are obtained from a plant, or part of a plant, that's used medicinally or therapeutically due to its properties. Herbs and spices form part of these botanical supplements. Herbs are the plant's leaves, while spices can be made from roots, stems, flowers, and seeds.

While herbs and spices are generally used for flavor, humans have used them for various functions for as long as people have been around. Ancient Egyptians had herbalist schools dating as far back as 3000 BCE. The Ebers Papyrus was a scroll from 1550 BCE that contained a list of medical remedies, including a wide range of botanicals. It's believed these botanicals have been traded for over 3,500 years. Before humans had pills, there were natural remedies, with botanicals containing the active ingredients that were later identified and became used in medications.

When using botanicals as supplements, you'll often find the plant's Latin name on the label, allowing you to be sure what you're consuming. Botanical supplements come in a range of formations. Not only are they used dried or fresh, but they are also used in ointments, tinctures, extracts, and so much more. The dose will determine the strength of the botanical supplement and the form it is in. Some forms are toxic to humans, like essential oils—which should never be consumed. So, while some fresh peppermint tea is ideal for a stomachache, consuming pure peppermint essential oil will be toxic.

Herbs

- **Basil** is high in vitamins and powerful antioxidants. It helps lower oxidative stress and the risk of cancer, diabetes, arthritis, and heart disease. Basil regulates blood sugar and lowers blood pressure, cholesterol, and inflammation. It's considered to have antibacterial properties.
- **Bay leaves** contain high levels of vitamins, minerals, fiber, and antioxidants. They boost the immune system, aid digestion, relieve a stuffy nose (when vapors are inhaled), and may even help lower blood sugar.
- **Chervil** is used to combat digestive issues, high blood pressure, gout, and skin conditions such as eczema. It can also soothe coughs.
- **Lemongrass** calms nerves, soothes gastrointestinal discomforts and joint pain, and lowers high blood pressure and cholesterol. It can also help lower fever and pain and fight against colds, coughs, and vomiting. As an antifungal (effective against ringworm), antiseptic, and astringent— it's used in lotions to soothe skin conditions. It's a great mosquito repellant.
- **Marjoram** contains antioxidants and has anti-inflammatory and antimicrobial properties. It may help soothe stomach ulcers. It might regulate irregular menstrual cycles and could even help alleviate symptoms of polycystic ovary syndrome (PCOS).
- **Oregano** is high in antioxidants, helping to improve resistance against infections, fight cancers, lower inflammation, regulate blood sugar, and assist in diminishing insulin resistance.

- **Parsley** is high in antioxidants and vitamins and boosts the immune system.
- **Peppermint** is antibacterial and aids in digestion. It's also a bronchodilator, which opens up airways and helps improve heart and lung health. Peppermint can also help guard against the pain associated with irritable bowel syndrome (IBS) and ease nausea. The smell of peppermint is enough to boost many people's moods.
- Smelling **rosemary** is enough to increase alertness, boost mood, and enliven brain function. Antispasmodic (helping prevent bronchial asthma) stimulates hair growth and has some preventive benefits against Alzheimer's disease. Rosemary also prevents ischemic heart disease, inflammatory diseases, peptic ulcers, atherosclerosis, liver toxicity, cataracts, and bacterial and yeast infections.
- **Sage** has been used to soothe sore throats, boost mood and memory, and help fight against diabetes and high cholesterol.
- **Savory** helps soothe gastrointestinal distress (stomach pain, gas, and diarrhea) and can also deal with coughs and loss of appetite. It has antispasmodic, antibacterial, and antifungal properties.
- **Thyme** is a powerful antioxidant and has antibacterial and antifungal properties. It aids in detoxifying the liver.

Spices

- Also known as pimento, **allspice** can be used to treat indigestion. It helps to soothe the symptoms of menopause and pain from menstruation, headaches, or toothaches. It's anti-inflammatory and has anticancer, antimicrobial, and antifungal properties. Allspice helps weight maintenance by reducing feelings of hunger and increasing the sensation of fullness. It improves insulin production, therefore helping to manage blood sugar levels.

- **Anise** has antidepressant, antifungal, and antibacterial properties. It protects against stomach ulcers, helps prevent bone loss, lowers inflammation, and helps to maintain blood sugar levels. Compounds in anise seeds mimic estrogen and can help relieve symptoms of menopause.
- **Ashwagandha** has been used to treat arthritis, infertility, and even diabetes. Ashwagandha also helps fight against fatigue, stress, and anxiety, boosting cognitive performance. It can be used to soothe back and muscle pain.
- **Black pepper** is created by cooking dried, unripe fruit. Pepper contains the compound piperine, known to lower the risk of cancers affecting the prostate, digestive tract, ovaries, and lungs.
- **Boswellia** is a resin from the frankincense tree often used to treat pain in joints and muscles. It is an effective treatment for pain and poor mobility for osteoarthritis patients. Creams containing Boswellia can even help soothe painful skin damage from radiation treatment.
- **Capsaicin** (the compound that makes chilis spicy) is known to regulate metabolic and heart health. Also known to assist in weight reduction by increasing fat metabolism, it reduces abdominal fat and is an appetite suppressant. All these factors together will aid weight loss. It's high in anti-inflammatory properties. Paprika and cayenne pepper also contain capsaicin.
- **Caraway seeds** are highly anti-inflammatory and soothe digestive issues like indigestion and stomach ulcers. They can promote changes in gut bacteria. This leads to positive

changes in appetite, such as improved feelings of fullness and decreased feelings of hunger and improves fat metabolism and hormone regulation.

- **Cardamom** is analgesic, antispasmodic, antimicrobial, and anti-inflammatory. Known to help fight heart disease and gastrointestinal issues like diarrhea and indigestion, cardamom also soothes headaches.
- High in many different minerals that help support strong bones, **celery seeds** help produce red blood cells and improve blood sugar levels—lowering the risk of type 2 diabetes and heart disease. Celery seeds also help enhance the sensitivity of cells to insulin. They have antibacterial properties.
- **Cinnamon** has antimicrobial, antidiabetic, and anticarcinogenic properties. High in antioxidants, it is anti-inflammatory. It's been used to lower blood sugar levels, improve cognitive function, and help lower blood pressure.
- **Cloves** are high in antioxidants and help to lower inflammation (especially in arthritis). The spice is high in beta-carotene, used to make vitamin A, and is suitable for the eyes.
- **Coriander** is the seed of the cilantro plant. The seeds are high in antioxidants, help protect against cancers and cognitive decline, and even soothe anxiety.
- **Cumin seeds** are high in antioxidants and help manage weight, stress, and cholesterol.
- **Devil's claw** helps soothe pain from tendonitis, an injured back and neck, and osteoarthritis. Good for pain relief, it is anti-inflammatory. It helps to decrease the symptoms of arthritis, improving quality of life.
- In the past, **dill seeds** were used to soothe colic in babies, treat digestive issues in adults, and improve breastfeeding.

High in antioxidants, dill seeds have anti-inflammatory, anticancer, antiviral, antifungal, and antibacterial properties. They help lower blood sugar levels, improve bone health, and lower pain from menstrual cramps.

- **Echinacea** helps to boost the immune system and aids in fighting colds.
- **Fenugreek** treats diabetes by helping lower blood sugar, increase milk flow, and relieve pain from menstrual cramps.
- Adding **garlic** to meals will help lower blood pressure and even boost the immune system enough to fight against colds.
- **Ginger** helps with gastrointestinal issues and is often used in controlling nausea. It's high in antioxidants and anti-inflammatory. It soothes pain associated with migraines, menstruation, and arthritis.
- High in antioxidants, **horseradish** has antibacterial, antifungal, and anticancer effects (it inhibits cancer-cell growth and may promote their death). It also helps relieve breathing issues and colds.
- Also known as Javitri, **mace spice** is the net-like covering on the shell outside the nutmeg seed. It's used to soothe pain (especially menstrual cramps) and alleviate stomach problems such as digestive issues, diarrhea, gas, and vomiting. It can assist in increasing menstrual flow, improving bladder control, and helping with mild gum disease. Mace spice has antibacterial, anticancer, and antifungal properties.
- **Mustard** can be consumed as seeds or a powder. It's high in minerals, antioxidants, and vitamins. Mustard has anticancer, anti-inflammatory, antibacterial, and antifungal properties. It helps lower blood sugar and boosts healing.

- **Nutmeg** contains powerful antioxidants with anti-inflammatory and antibacterial properties. It's specifically powerful against oral and *E. coli* infections.
- **Saffron** may help with eye improvement in adults suffering from age-related macular degeneration (AMD) and improve cognitive function in adults with Alzheimer's disease. This antioxidant helps as an antidepressant while protecting the brain and lowering inflammation and appetite, which leads to weight loss. It helps to improve mood, fight against mild-to-moderate depression, and reduce symptoms of post-menstrual stress. It even has aphrodisiac properties—especially for people with low sex drive as a result of being on antidepressants.
- **Star anise** has anti-inflammatory and antimicrobial properties and is high in antioxidants. It helps to support the immune system, eases coughs and bronchitis, and promotes digestive health by relieving symptoms of indigestion.
- **Tarragon** treats fevers and upper respiratory infections, soothes stomach ulcers, aids digestion, and stimulates appetite. It can also help make new fat cells and influence glucose and insulin levels in people with diabetes.
- Known to have anti-inflammatory properties, **turmeric** helps fight against viral, bacterial, and parasitic infections. It can be used to help lower the risk of type 2 diabetes, arthritis, and metabolic syndrome. Curcumin, the anti-inflammatory compound in turmeric, isn't very bioavailable. To help the absorption of curcumin, add some black pepper, as piperine helps with the absorption of curcumin.
- **White pepper** is made by cooking and drying the ripe seeds. Often used to treat gastrointestinal issues (upset

stomach and diarrhea), white pepper helps decrease pain and inflammation and improves brain function.

- **White willow bark** contains a compound known as salicin, which is used to produce aspirin. This natural remedy is often used to deal with inflammation and pain, including muscular and joint pain.

Probiotics and Digestive Enzymes

Probiotics and digestive enzymes are great for improving your digestive and gut health. Though both give similar results, they aren't the same thing.

Probiotics are living microbes often called cultures. They can be consumed as supplements or in probiotic foods such as yogurt, kimchi, and tempeh. Their function is to maintain the level of excellent and pathogenic microbes in your gut.

While different probiotics and digestive enzymes can be consumed together—as they address problems such as gas, bloating, and irregular bowel movements—other symptoms will suggest which supplement is better.

There are numerous benefits to adding probiotics and digestive enzymes to your diet.

Probiotics

Probiotics can help against autoimmune disorders, chronic fatigue, metabolic syndrome, and more. Generally, probiotics are used to fix intestinal conditions, including colon cancer, IBS, and inflammatory bowel disease (IBD). However, with time, this can also lead to the healing of non-intestinal disorders.

Take probiotics if you have:

- mood issues (anxiety or irritability)
- skin problems (acne, eczema, or rashes)
- low concentration
- bad breath
- fatigue
- sore or poor joint health
- vaginal or rectal itching or infection
- weak immune system

Lactobacillus and *Bifidobacterium* are two of the most common groups associated with probiotics, but within these groups are many different species, giving a variety of benefits. These benefits include lowering inflammation, increasing high-density lipoproteins (HDL or good cholesterol), improving blood sugar levels, reducing oxidative stress damage, helping fight against cancer, decreasing bowel issues, and even reducing liver inflammation. A healthy gut will boost your immune system and limit the invasion of pathogenic microbes.

However, when taking antibiotics or eating a poor diet, many microbes die—the good and the bad. The pathogenic microbes multiply quickly and will take over the gut microbiome if fresh probiotics aren't added. This imbalance of microbes causes inflammation in the gut and, when chronic, can lead to a variety of diseases such as type 2 diabetes, chronic fatigue, and obesity.

Digestive Enzymes

The body requires digestive enzymes to help make food more manageable and absorbable so it can produce energy. In most cases, people won't have a problem with their digestive enzymes.

However, those with pancreatic cancer, chronic pancreatitis, cystic fibrosis, or who have experienced several gastrointestinal surgeries may require digestive enzymes to help with breaking down what they eat. When given digestive enzyme supplements, these people can process their food better and improve their absorption. Digestive enzymes are also provided to help with the treatment of IBS. The benefits of digestive enzymes include alleviating gut irritation, bloating, gas, acid reflux, and heartburn.

Digestive enzymes are chemicals that break down complex nutrients into smaller, more easily digestible components. This allows them to cross the gut-blood barrier more easily. The body has different digestive enzymes that target specific types of food:

- **Amylase** is made in the salivary glands and breaks carbohydrates into simple sugars.
- **Lactase** is made in the small intestine and breaks down lactose into glucose and galactose.
- **Lipase** is made in the pancreas and breaks fat into fatty acids and glycerol.
- **Protease** is made in the pancreas and breaks proteins into amino acids.
- **Sucrase** is made in the small intestine and changes sucrose into glucose and fructose.

Digestive enzymes can also be found in food such as mango, kiwi, avocado, and ginger or taken as a supplement under doctor's orders. There is no reason a healthy person will even need digestive enzyme supplements unless otherwise stated by a doctor.

Take digestive enzymes if you have:

- an uncomfortable feeling after meals
- food sensitivities
- frequent burping
- indigestion or acid reflux
- nausea
- oily stool
- sudden, unexpected weight loss

RISKS AND CONSIDERATIONS OF SUPPLEMENTS

Regardless of which type, the FDA does not regulate supplements, despite some containing powerful active ingredients often used in pharmaceutical drugs. Some risks are associated with taking supplements because there isn't a way to determine the strength of their active ingredients.

These active ingredients can interact with those in pharmaceutical drugs, alternative medications, or other supplements—leading to side effects. You may never know how much of a vitamin, mineral, or active ingredient you are taking daily—especially when combined with enriched or fortified foods, where extra minerals and vitamins are added. You may be getting far more than you should! With some vitamins and minerals, there isn't an upper limit; in others, there is, each leading to their own toxicity symptom.

Here are just some of the problems you can run into:

- **Iron and calcium:** High levels of these will lower the effectiveness of antibiotics.
- **St. John's wort:** This botanical can reduce the efficacy of some drugs, includ2ing birth control and antidepressants.

- **Vitamin A:** Taking this vitamin alongside Accutane or Soriatane will result in a headache, rash, nausea, and vomiting.
- **Vitamin B6:** Using excessive vitamin B6 for a year or more will result in severe nerve damage and decrease the effectiveness of Dilantin (an anti-seizure drug) and Levodopa (a Parkinson's medication).
- **Vitamin C:** While vitamin C is quickly washed from the body—as it's water soluble—consuming excessive amounts will result in diarrhea.
- **Vitamin E:** This vitamin can increase the effectiveness of blood thinners, leading to more bruising and possible nose bleeds.
- **Vitamin K:** This vitamin can lower the effectiveness of warfarin in slowing blood clotting.

Older people can easily find themselves in danger from these interactions and side effects. Once over 60, people tend to take more medication and supplements, both of which they struggle to metabolize as they used to, meaning they tend to take more than what is usually required. With filter organs—such as the liver and kidneys—not functioning at peak, it becomes more difficult to flush the body of the supplements, increasing the odds of negative interactions.

Some argue that supplements labeled "natural" are better for people, but this isn't true. They contain the same active ingredients that can interact with other medications and supplements. Believing they are harmless is dangerous—especially to people who rely on medicine, such as anti-rejection medications, to stay alive.

While wading through the vast number of supplements and medications available, it can be a chore to determine the safest way to choose the right one for you. So, here are a few safety tips to allow you to make the right choice and avoid any possible interactions:

- ▷ Always know what you're taking (medication, supplements, etc.). Create a list and keep it with you. When you go to your doctor, you can give it to them so they can check for possible interactions.
- ▷ Inform your doctor of any health changes—an illness, an upcoming surgery, or a pregnancy.
- ▷ When getting new medication, be sure to ask:
  - "Should anything be avoided while on this medication?"
  - "Are there any drug interactions?"
  - "What will this drug do to me?"
- ▷ Research the possible drug interactions of any medication you are advised to take. Sites like RxList (https://www.rxlist.com/) are a great way to find warning labels you can discuss with your doctor.
- ▷ Read the labels of all medications and supplements, prescribed or over the counter, before taking them.
- ▷ It's a good idea to stick to a specific pharmacy when getting your medication, as this will make it easier to keep track of what you're on.

Never be afraid to discuss your medication and supplements with your health practitioner but realize that supplements will be unlikely to replace a healthy, well-balanced diet.

TIPS FOR INCORPORATING SUPPLEMENTS INTO A SELF-HEALING PLAN

In the same way that a doctor produces a treatment plan, you can develop your self-healing plan with these steps:

1. Create a plan.

a. Know what supplements you need for your age and circumstances (e.g., fighting chronic diseases or pain). Please speak to a doctor about what they suggest is best for you.

2. Follow the label's instructions.

a. Unless instructed by a doctor to take a specific dosage, follow the instructions on the supplement facts label.

3. Consider when to take supplements.

a. Depending on the supplement you're taking, certain times of the day may be better than others, while other supplements may require you to take them with food.

i. Fat-soluble vitamins are best consumed with a meal or snack that contains healthy fats, like avocado or nuts.
ii. Iron supplements are best consumed with orange juice or other vitamin C drinks.
iii. Magnesium supports relaxation and is best taken before bed.
iv. Vitamin B complex provides energy, so take these in the morning.

v. Water-soluble vitamins should be taken with a glass of water at mealtimes.

4. Have a routine.

a. Supplements need to be taken consistently to work correctly and should be incorporated into your daily routine.
b. Pick a specific time(s) to take your supplements and place them in an easily noticed area so you don't forget.

5. Get organized.

a. There is an array of organizing tools available, from pill boxes to baskets, to help separate the various medications you may be on. These tools will let you notice when your supplies are dwindling and need replacing.
b. Consider getting an extra bottle or container of supplements so you don't run out but keep an eye on the expiration date.

6. Patience is needed.

a. The results of taking supplements aren't instantaneous, and it can take weeks to months before you notice them.
b. Pairing supplements with a healthier lifestyle, a nutritious diet, exercise, and quality sleep may speed up the process.

7. Choose quality supplements.

a. While the FDA does not regulate most supplements, they can be verified. Always choose products that are United

States Pharmacopoeia (USP) verified or have at least been tested and verified by a third party.

One of the root causes of many different chronic diseases and pain is a poor diet. Taking the time to change what you eat will help you heal from the inside out. However, a diet can be lacking in something for many different reasons, and various supplements can be used to supplement these possible deficiencies. Herbs and other botanicals are anti-inflammatory and rich in vitamins and minerals to strengthen the body, boost immune systems, and lower inflammation responses. As long as you give your body all it needs, it can heal itself.

In the next chapter, we'll explore the mindfulness's effect on the body regarding self-healing and managing chronic diseases and pain.

CHAPTER THREE

FINDING PEACE WITHIN

MINDFULNESS, MEDITATION, SELF-AWARENESS, AND EMOTIONAL INTELLIGENCE TO SELF-HEAL AND MANAGE CHRONIC DISEASES AND PAIN

A few years ago, I was approached by a client at the end of their rope. They had been diagnosed with fibromyalgia a few months previously and could no longer take the pain they were going through. They worked a highly stressful job, and the pain was making it too difficult for them to work. Their friend recommended me, and they truly felt I was their last option. They had already made changes to their diet to help lower inflammation but still found it too difficult with the pain.

Fibromyalgia is a disorder caused by repeated stimulation of nerves due to abnormal pain-signaling chemicals in the brain. This causes widespread muscular pain throughout the body, leading to fatigue, cognitive issues, and problems with sleep, mood, and memory.

I took the time to teach them how mindfulness and meditation could help with their condition. They agreed to try it, as they saw no other way out. However, after a few days, they called me in desperation, saying it wasn't working. After listening for a few minutes, I asked them if they had noticed any positives while trying the mindful techniques. After a brief silence, they rattled some off. After talking a little longer, I suggested they extend their mindfulness sessions and concentrate on the now, not overthinking their pain. I remember the scoff of disbelief as they hung up. I didn't hear from them for several days and was concerned that something had happened, but then the phone rang.

My patient was still experiencing the pain from their fibromyalgia, but it wasn't nearly as bad as before. Focusing on the now allowed them to concentrate on the pain and emotionally deal with it. This also allowed them to realize they were more than their disease. They knew they still had a lot of work to do, but my guidance and patience in teaching them mindfulness had helped them on the road to using it to help deal with their pain.

UNDERSTANDING MINDFULNESS

Mindfulness isn't mind over matter; it's something deeper. Mindfulness is a person's ability to be aware of everything around them without becoming overwhelmed or judgmental. Mindfulness is made up of three factors. The first is intention: when people know why they're practicing mindfulness. The second is attention: the focus on the now. The final factor is acceptance: the ability to observe what is being felt without passing judgment.

Mindfulness allows you to concentrate on yourself, changing how your brain focuses and functions. Brains shift in response to what they experience—negative or positive—and which one you focus on will change your life. Mindfulness isn't something that happens; it takes practice and time to make the effects necessary to improve your life. However, once you make the breakthrough, there are many benefits. According to research, mindfulness can improve heart health, sleep, mood, focus, and self-confidence. It can also decrease feelings of anxiety, stress, depression, and pain.

Chronic illnesses and pain are often caused by high levels of stress, which induce inflammation and lower the immune system. By dealing with this stress, chronic conditions can be combated over time. Mindfulness, together with meditation, can have an impact on the intensity and perception of pain. Pain can be difficult to quantify, as each person perceives it differently, which is why mindfulness is such a crucial tool because it can be individualized. Meditation can play a vital role as it lets a person explore the present moment, allowing them to concentrate on sensations, emotions, and thoughts—honestly, within that moment.

The weather, psychology, and cognition can influence how pain is felt. Mindfulness helps with how the brain processes pain and how a person reacts to it. It isn't a cure, but it changes your relationship between pain and reaction. While there is significant anecdotal evidence for mindfulness helping with chronic conditions, there is also a lot of research that shows people can self-regulate chronic pain and decrease their experience of it and how they perceive it. They can even reduce their pain sensitivity. Some studies show that mindfulness therapies can improve the symptoms of chronic lower back pain, while yoga and meditative practices can help lower inflammation in white blood cells. As inflammation can lead to pain, dealing with the cause can address the symptoms.

People who go through cancer treatment are often plagued with pain, sleeplessness, and poor health—but with a combination of mindfulness and meditation, they can improve their mental health. By boosting mental health, sleep improves, pain is perceived at a lower rate, and there's a decrease in discomfort and anxiety. Chronic conditions, such as insomnia and obesity, can also be handled with mindfulness—allowing you to get the rest you need and manage to eat healthier, leading to sustainable weight loss.

There are a variety of mindfulness techniques that can be used to help with chronic illness. Regardless of which method or therapy is used, mindfulness is aimed at increasing a sense of well-being and improving quality of life.

Mindfulness can help in many different ways to fight back against chronic diseases and pain:

Mindfulness encourages self-care, self-compassion, and self-love.

- Don't focus on the problems you're going through. Instead, focus your energy on taking care of yourself by knowing your needs and how to meet them.
- Be supportive of yourself, even when in pain or distress, whether it is due to your own actions or those of outside forces.

It inspires you to surround yourself with goodness.

- Learn to surround yourself with support, love, and inspiration while rejecting all toxic influences. While this may be difficult—especially if the toxic influences are people—it will help improve your health.

It helps you become more receptive and aware of other healthy options.

- A mind clouded by pain easily misses opportunities and makes poor judgments. Grounding yourself allows you to review all the pros and cons of the various treatment options before making a choice.

Learn how to silence your inner critic and be compassionate toward yourself.

- We all have an inner voice, some more negative than others. Learn to ignore the negative inner voice and show yourself some compassion. You may be disappointed with where you are, but you still have much to offer the world, so share!

Discover how to control your pain.

- Practicing mindfulness with meditation leads to the release of endorphins, which are chemicals that are natural painkillers.

Mindfulness boosts gratitude.

- At this very moment, there are many things to be grateful for, no matter how small and insignificant you may think they are. Noticing all these things will help shift your well-being into a better place.

It motivates you to let go of *what-ifs*.

- Stay in the present and find ways to thrive as you are now. While your envisioned future may never be what you always hoped it could be, you can still make the most of it! Learn to let go.

Mindfulness prevents you from being defined by your illness.

- You are a unique person with many gifts to share, so focus on everything that brings you joy, not your disease or pain.

Be reminded that you're human; embrace and accept this.

- Illness is part of the human condition. We are fragile and mortal. You can't control everything, so accept what you cannot, learn to focus on what you can manage, and be mindful.

It teaches you that helping yourself helps others.

- Focusing on the present brings your focus closer to you and what's happening around you. Helping others can be a powerful healing source and solace to you and others.

FOOD FOR THOUGHT: MINDFUL EATING

While a healthy diet is vital to your health, how you eat your food is just as important. Mindful eating is being aware of how you eat, paying attention to your food, experiencing each bite, savoring the moment, and enjoying it. Unlike a diet that may limit how much or what you can eat, mindful eating lets you eat what your body tells you to eat. It's all about focusing on the experience. When incorporating mindful eating, you'll find that you're eating less, savoring the flavors more, and selecting more foods to boost your health. Mindful eating allows you to appreciate everything about your meals: the appearance, texture, smell, and taste.

Using physical and emotional senses, you will get to experience food in a whole different light. It's rare that people sit and enjoy a meal for the sake of enjoying it. We're all too busy and rushed to have sit-down meals without being distracted by our phones, the TV, or work. Eating food should be enjoyable, not a chore or an opportunity to pass judgment on yourself. Being aware of what you're putting on your plate and into your mouth will lead to making better choices in your food shopping.

Mindful eating allows you to focus on the experience of eating, listening to body-related sensations (i.e., hungry or sated). It will enable you to consider your thoughts and feelings about what you're eating and become aware of everything without feeling judgment over what you're eating. There are seven practices for mindful eating:

1. Honor the food you're consuming by eating without distractions and acknowledge where the food came from and who prepared it. Appreciate the food between each bite.
2. Draw upon all your senses to enjoy what you're eating.
3. Use a smaller plate, about nine inches in diameter, to practice moderation.
4. Enjoy smaller bites and savor each one by thoroughly chewing.
5. Eat slowly and listen to your body's cues. Stop eating when you're about 80% full to prevent yourself from overeating.
6. Take your time; there is no need to rush.
7. Never skip a meal, as this can make you hungrier than necessary. However, if you do, then eat your next meal being mindful.

8. Experiment with plant-based meals to help lower your intake of saturated fats while increasing your intake of fiber, vitamins, and minerals.

Mindful eating doesn't start when you put food on your plate; it begins when you're shopping. To avoid making poor choices, stay within the fresh food aisle and avoid traveling toward the center aisles. These areas tend to have prepackaged goods containing ingredients that may induce inflammation. Make sure you have a shopping list handy, so you only get precisely what you need for the week or month and do your best to avoid unnecessary spending on food you don't need.

By learning to read your body cues, you can prevent overeating. This can be difficult, primarily if you've been raised to clean your plate at every meal or you're a stress eater. Learned behaviors around food influence how we eat, such as forcing ourselves to finish plates when we're not hungry or starving ourselves when it's not mealtime yet. Stress can also cause overeating, as the brain interprets stress as the body undergoing a famine. Instead of reaching for healthy foods during stressful times, the brain demands foods high in salt, sugar, and fat, as these provide an instant *good feeling*.

Overeating, regardless of the reason, will eventually lead to insulin resistance, metabolic syndrome, type 2 diabetes, and obesity—not to mention how certain foods can cause increased inflammation, leading to other chronic conditions.

Being mindful of food comes with many benefits. It allows you to appreciate the food you eat, curbs cravings, regulates eating patterns (e.g., decreases snacking), increases digestion by chewing better, fosters a positive attitude toward food, and helps with weight loss as it reduces overeating and binging.

Mindful eating teaches you to listen to your gut. It tells you when you're hungry and when you're full. Please don't ignore it; strive to unlearn bad eating habits where you're forced to eat everything.

Eating mindfully teaches you what your body needs by helping you realize what foods and quantities of that food are required to get you through your day. Awareness starts when you're shopping, not when you open the fridge door.

You can even discover a new awareness of what you're doing when you're eating. Many people have emotional attachments to food. Now is the time to free yourself from any negative attachments you may have and relish creating new mindful connections to what you eat. Mindful eating isn't the only way to bring calm to yourself and improve your health.

MEDITATION TECHNIQUES THAT CULTIVATE MINDFULNESS

Meditation is another tool that can help you reach mindfulness. Meditation is a collection of practices focusing on concentration and living in the moment. It has been practiced for centuries, was developed during the *Vedic* times, and is still practiced by millions today. Not many people can meditate, and some get more anxious trying. However, starting small and then extending your meditation time will help give you a better experience.

Mindfulness meditation is aimed at changing your mindset and perspective, which, in turn, can help rewire the brain for more positive emotions and thoughts. Doing this allows you to feel less fear, stress, and anxiety. Practicing daily will allow you to not only manage your worry but also increase your compassion and empathy, bringing focus to your life while learning patience and revitalizing yourself. While some people can start this mindfulness journey alone, others can't. Instead of getting frustrated over not reaching your meditation goals, try a few guided meditations to help you with the basics. There are different techniques you can use.

Focused Meditation

Focused meditation is when you focus on something that enables you to remain within the current moment. It helps to slow down the mindless chatter of your inner voice and allows you to focus on your breathing or one of your senses.

This meditation comes with many benefits. It'll help improve concentration, attention, and focus—allowing you to concentrate through distraction while enabling you to regulate your emotions more quickly because you have improved your response to internal feelings.

To attempt this, find a comfortable place where you are sitting with a straight back. Prop yourself up if needed, and if you're more comfortable sitting cross-legged, do so:

1. Choose what you want to focus on. Breathing is generally a good start, but you can use your senses if you want to.
2. Start to relax your shoulders and breathe from your belly. You may get sleepy when you start, but this will improve with more practice.
3. Concentrate on what you want to focus on and all the sensations that come with it. When concentrating on breathing, feel the air pull through your nose, enter your lungs, extend your belly, etc.

4. In the beginning, you may find your inner voice surfaces. Don't feel frustrated; this is normal. Rein it in by returning your attention to your focus to quieten your mind. Noticing a noisy mind isn't a sign of failure; it's a victory that you recognize it. Acknowledge that it is there and re-establish your focus.
5. Start with short sessions lasting a few minutes and be kind to yourself as you learn.

This meditation isn't for everyone, so if it isn't working, try a different technique and revisit it when you're ready.

Body Scan

The body scan technique allows you to pinpoint areas on your body that are under discomfort: tension, pain, or aches. This technique doesn't aim to relieve the pain but to acknowledge that it's there and to help you manage it better in the future.

It allows you to lower your stress levels and helps fight against psychological and physical tensions:

1. Start by lying in a comfortable position.
2. Allow your belly to breathe, concentrating on it being the only part of you moving.
3. Then, start scanning your body, beginning with your feet. While focusing on your feet, sense if any sensations are associated with them. If there are, focus on any tension or pain you're experiencing.
4. Breathe into any discomfort you're feeling. Allow yourself to visualize the tension being relieved and breathed out of

your body. Concentrate on your feet until you're ready to move on to the next section of your body.

5. Continue this practice from your feet to your head, concentrating on specific body parts and breathing the tension out as you move through your body. With practice, this technique allows you to easily release tension and pain over time.

This can be abbreviated when you're short on time, though this is only suggested once you've acclimatized to the complete method. The abbreviated version allows you to carry out the technique while seated and concentrating on one specific body part instead of doing the whole scan.

Breathing Exercises

There are many breathing exercises you can try. While they are all different, their benefits are similar. Meditative breathing allows you to lower your anxiety, depression, and stress levels while improving your sleep quality, motor memory, and pain processing.

4-7-8 Technique

The 4-7-8 breathing technique is a counting technique that lowers stress and anxiety using controlled breathing. It's based on pranayama breathing, which is often used in relaxation for yoga. It helps to activate the parasympathetic nervous system to aid relaxation:

1. Sit in a quiet place and relax.
2. Position your tongue against the back of your front teeth.
3. Open your mouth and breathe out.

4. Close your mouth and inhale through your nose for four seconds.
5. Hold your breath for seven seconds.
6. Exhale with your mouth open and tongue behind your front teeth for eight seconds. The breath coming out should make a whooshing noise. It should feel that you have no more air in your lungs when you're done.
7. Breathe in once more and allow for four cycles.

This technique can be practiced up to twice a day, and once you are comfortable with it, you can go up to eight cycles. You must sit in a quiet place to focus on your breathing.

Belly Breathing

This is a type of abdominal breathing technique that focuses on lowering stress and anxiety:

1. Sit or lie down in a comfortable position.
2. Place one hand on your chest and the other on your belly, just below the rib cage.
3. Clench your stomach muscles and breathe out.
4. Breathe in, allowing the belly muscles to expand while the chest remains unmoving.
5. Breathe out through pursed lips. Keep your chest from moving while the belly is pulled back toward the spine.

Box Breathing

This technique is a form of paced breathing where breathing in, holding breath, and breathing out takes four seconds each:

1. Sit in a comfortable position and breathe out for four seconds.
2. Keep your lungs empty for four seconds.
3. Inhale for four seconds.
4. Hold your breath for four seconds.
5. Start the cycle again.

There are a variety of other breathing exercises, so if these are of no help to you, explore the alternatives to see which helps you best.

Loving-Kindness

Loving-kindness is a self-caring technique to improve your well-being and lower stress. It also increases your capacity to forgive, have self-acceptance, and aid in connecting better with others. Mastering this technique allows you to focus on giving and receiving loving energy. This technique can be complex for many people as they aren't used to giving and receiving love at a high magnitude.

This technique is highly beneficial to those with high anxiety or anger or who are prone to conflicts. It also reduces stress in those giving long-term care to others. Practicing this technique helps to increase empathy while lowering negativity and rumination over negative thoughts:

1. Sit somewhere quiet; get comfortable before closing your eyes and relax your muscles as you take a few deep breaths.
2. Imagine yourself being truly at inner peace. You love who you are now, and you're thanking yourself for being *you*.

Breathe out all the tensions you're feeling and breathe in love and appreciation.

3. You can repeat several positive and reassuring phrases (or mantras) as you go through the exercise. Try phrases such as: "May I be loved.", "May I give and receive love today.", "May I be strong and resilient."
4. Enjoy the feelings of self-compassion. If you feel your focus deviating, focus on breathing in love or directing compassion to others you are close to. These are the ones you want to share love with. You can even extend these compassionate feelings to everyone and beyond—even those you don't particularly like.
5. Continue with the meditation until you believe it's over. You can shift from this meditation to breathing meditation before finishing your session.

How a person meditates is deeply personal, so if you find none of these techniques work for you, seek out others and explore them until you discover those that work.

Meditation Anchors and How They Deepen Mindfulness Meditation

If you have never tried meditation, one of the biggest frustrations is remaining within the moment and not allowing your mind to wander. This happens to everyone, and it will take some time to prevent the inner voice from chatting away or becoming distracted. You'll have to develop a few anchors to help prevent these distractions reducing your benefits. An anchor allows your mind to focus once it becomes distracted. Anchors will also help to improve meditation and even encourage adherence and persistence of meditation, according to Stecher et al. (2021).

You can use many kinds of anchors, but the most common is your breathing. While breathing, you can focus on all the sensations involved in breathing, such as the temperature of the air coming into your lungs versus what you are breathing out. You can even concentrate on the duration of your breathing and how long the breath can be held in your lungs.

You don't need to rely solely on your breath. You can use a body anchor. As you're sitting or lying down, you can concentrate on the pressure and temperature created at the points where you make contact with what you're lying or sitting on.

Sensation anchors allow you to use bodily or external sensations to help you focus during meditation. Something as simple as listening or feeling your heartbeat is enough of an anchor to keep you focused. When practicing meditation outdoors, you can use the feeling of sunlight on your skin (be careful not to burn), the wind across your skin, or even the scent of flowers in your garden. Using smell as an anchor can be challenging, as human noses tend to become desensitized to smells over time.

Sound anchors are another great way to focus. People can use chants, sound bowls, or natural sounds to help them remain focused. When using a natural sound, ensure it is a noise that is always in the background, as this makes it easier to sharpen your focus. While wind through the trees can be soothing, the wind may die down eventually. Instead, concentrate on a ticking clock or even the hum of your fridge.

Mantras can also be used as an anchor. Many people prefer to avoid using mantras as they can be associated with specific religions or be in languages that are difficult to understand. However, there's no reason to use these particular mantras—especially when you can make your own. Consider the loving-kindness mantras and make your ones that foster a positive belief system and easy to repeat when needed.

There is no reason to have a single anchor. Many people have a foreground anchor and several others in the background, allowing them to switch—as needed—for their meditative sessions.

Intrusive thoughts and distractions will occur. Use your main anchor to get yourself focused on your meditation and mindfulness. If this anchor doesn't work, switch to the others you have. This will give you the focus to collect your thoughts and sharpen your concentration. Anchors must be pleasant and create a neutral feeling.

INCORPORATING MINDFULNESS IN DAILY LIFE

Mindfulness doesn't need to take up hours of your day. Many mindfulness techniques only take a few minutes. Daily reflections are very helpful in bringing focus, relaxation, and increased alertness. There are hundreds of ways to bring mindfulness into your life right now as you're reading this book. Mindful reading allows you to truly concentrate on the words you're reading without being distracted by anything outside your book's pages. Knowing how to carry out these micro-practices of mindfulness instead of doing a full meditation is a good idea. Here are a few easy ways you can incorporate mindfulness into a day without feeling overwhelmed:

Focus on your breathing.

- When the negativity in your life gets a little too much, take the time to breathe a few deep breaths. Focus on all the sensations of breathing. It would be best if you refocused yourself this way.

- Take five full belly breaths, concentrating on the inhalation and exhalation, and repeat three times.

Focus on your tasks.

- The hustle and bustle of modern life has too many distractions, making it difficult to focus. Slow down when doing tasks. This allows you to do things more deliberately and with purpose, giving the task all the attention it deserves. Incorporate all your senses while you work. This can also be applied to mindful eating.

Focus on body awareness.

- Allow yourself to feel all the sensations of being alive. Notice everything around you by using all your senses, allow emotions to be present by labeling them as needed but *not* passing judgment, and acknowledge that you have urges and cravings by concentrating on feeling them but *not* feeding them.
- Many things happen automatically in the body. There are sensations to feel and hear and tensions and pains to address. Bring attention to these parts that need focus.

Practice gratitude daily.

- Focus on all the positives in your life, always bringing them to the forefront of your thoughts. Don't concern yourself with the future, and don't dwell on the past. Focus on the *now*.

Listen to your heart.

- Emotions affect your heart and make it beat differently. Take the time to listen to your heart when you're confused by feelings and allow yourself time to understand what you're feeling.

Use all your senses.

- Pause in your day to allow yourself to feel the *now* with all your senses. Indeed, observe everything around you.

Center yourself.

- The world is chaotic; sometimes, you need to center your inner self and release tension. Allow your eyes to close where you're standing or sitting, keeping a straight back, and start a body scan from your head to your toes. Release any tension you find through your body into the ground as you concentrate on breathing. Once you feel better, continue with your day.

Observe your thoughts.

- It's easy to get caught up in negative thoughts. Pause and observe your feelings and allow your thoughts to lead you. Acknowledge what they are, and don't pass judgment.

Try active listening.

- Instead of spacing out when people talk to you, concentrate on what they tell you. Give them your undying attention, and soon, you'll find your quality of conversations drastically improved.

Observe your surroundings.

- While a warning for some, this is a sure way to allow mindfulness while focusing on everything that happens around you.
- The world is full of wonders; allow your mind to latch onto them, experiencing everything to do with *this* wonder before moving on to the *next.* This mindfulness allows you to appreciate everything around you. Try this the next time you go for a walk.

There are a variety of ways you can bring mindfulness into your day. Try a gratitude list, where you add something you're grateful for daily. You can even try mindful gardening. This allows you to use all your senses while working in the garden, giving you a deeper connection with nature.

If you have youngsters who you want to teach mindfulness, why not try the senses scavenger hunt? Encourage the children to use their senses to identify one thing in their surroundings that has something to do with their various senses.

Mindfulness has a way of trickling down to others. When you're in a better place in your life, you tend to be more empathic and compassionate, leading to you dealing with difficult situations and people a lot better and, perhaps, even helping a few other people simultaneously.

There is no need to dedicate time to being mindful. Mindfulness can easily be incorporated into the most boring of daily tasks. Next time you're standing in a queue, waiting on public transport, heading to work, brushing your teeth, or doing chores—use all your senses to feel out the *now*, do some belly breathing, and center yourself. Why waste precious time going to the nothing box in your mind or getting frustrated when you could be spending that time being more mindful in everything you do?

Mindfulness is the key to helping you combat the various things that contribute to the risk factors of chronic diseases. While mindfulness doesn't cure these problems, it can help you get better at managing the conditions, building up a resistance to pain, becoming more tolerant, and—with mindful eating—making the right choice when it comes to your diet, lowering these risk factors even more. In the following chapter, we'll concentrate on the root cause of most chronic diseases and pain: gut health.

CHAPTER FOUR

IT ALL STARTS HERE

THE ROOT OF ALL CHRONIC DISEASES AND PAIN: POOR GUT HEALTH

Nearly 50% of Americans—roughly 133 million—are suffering from at least one chronic disease (Health for Life, 2007). The total of those with chronic diseases has risen by 15 million in the last ten years, and by the time 2030 rolls around, it's estimated that the total will increase to 170 million. This will have an impact on the health system, as well as wallets.

Most of your immune system is found along the gastrointestinal tract—meaning, if something goes wrong in the gastrointestinal tract, the immune system will respond quickly. Within the gastrointestinal tract are billions of microorganisms, also known as the microbiome, which work tirelessly on various jobs that improve your life. A strong microbiome is required for your health as it plays a role in nutrition, metabolism, and the immune system.

When the microbiome is in homeostasis, there is a balance between the different microorganisms. However, when the equilibrium is disturbed, dysbiosis occurs; this allows pathogenic microorganisms to flourish and cause problems, such as inflammatory or autoimmune diseases. One such problem is when the bacteria and their products escape the confinement of the gastrointestinal tract and bypass the gut lining. In the case of leaky gut syndrome, endotoxins released by bacteria can travel through the weakened gut lining, causing an immediate response from the immune system, leading to inflammation. If these toxins continue through the gut lining, the inflammation can become chronic, leading to various chronic conditions and pain.

However, the microbiome is constantly in flux, and the increase or decrease of specific microorganisms may not necessarily cause a condition; instead, they may be alerting you to a potential problem. Science is still exploring how the consistency of the microbiome can influence your health.

UNDERSTANDING CHRONIC DISEASES

A chronic disease continues for a minimum of three months but can last for years. It's often difficult to cope with a diagnosis of a chronic illness as, unlike other diseases, there is a low chance of getting a cure, despite constant doctor's visits to try new medications and therapies. The symptoms of chronic diseases often hamper life as they tend to get worse as the disease progresses.

A chronic disease isn't the same as an acute disease. An acute disease has a sudden onset of symptoms that tend to run their course, can be treated with medication, and will eventually be cured. Chronic diseases have a slow onset of symptoms that progressively worsen. However, acute diseases can become chronic when not correctly diagnosed and treated.

The characteristics of a chronic disease are that they tend to be driven by different types of risk factors with many complex causes

—it's rare to pinpoint the exact reason a chronic disease develops. A chronic disease isn't immediately noticed, as the symptoms start sometime after the disorder is triggered. A chronic disease cannot be managed naturally, and some intervention is required to address the symptoms. While some chronic diseases are life-threatening (e.g., cardiovascular diseases), most are manageable (like arthritis). All chronic diseases will cause some functional impairment or a disability.

The most common chronic diseases include, but aren't limited to, heart disease, metabolic disorder, type 2 diabetes, obesity, a variety of cancers (e.g., lung, colorectal), arthritis, Crohn's disease, chronic obstructive pulmonary disease (COPD), and chronic kidney disease (CKD), to name a few.

Living with a chronic condition can cause many different stresses in life that you'll need to come to terms with:

- There will be physical effects, including pain, illness, and mood changes.
- You will need to learn to manage your treatments in terms of cost and time.
- You must have excellent communication with your doctors, so they know of all your current medications and treatments.
- Negative feelings will start to creep up, and you'll need to manage them with various techniques.
- Trying to be positive and continue to have confidence may seem impossible, especially when you've been told there's no cure.

While there are many stresses you need to manage, it is possible. Don't let a diagnosis diminish your hopes of living a fulfilling life.

Many people are flourishing despite having chronic diseases. Regardless of wanting to have a cheery outlook, it's often difficult to do as there are no actual cures, only management of the symptoms.

The symptoms of a chronic disease are already taxing on the body, but these aren't the only demands on you and your health. Being sick all the time is stressful, and the more stress you suffer, the worse the disorder becomes; it could even herald the way for another chronic disease. Other demands include:

- Understanding the condition is enough to do your research. This will allow you to research different therapies and treatments available.
- Working with your doctor, remaining confident with their treatment plans, and trusting them, even when there is no cure in immediate sight.
- Figuring out different ways to deal with the myriad of symptoms.
- Trying your best not to avoid social interactions. Strong relationships and support networks should be in place when you're at your lowest.

Each chronic disease has different symptoms and treatment options; therefore, the effects on your life will be different from those of someone else going through the same thing. Chronic diseases have many characteristics, some of which are invisible, such as pain, fatigue, and mood changes, while others will have physical changes, such as increased weight or noticeable inflammation. Some of these changes cause you to lose self-esteem, pulling you away from others and affecting your social life. In other cases, the pain and stiffness can affect your previous range of motion, making it difficult to do everything you once did. These physical limitations affect your life and can be detrimental to your job. The fear and stress of losing your career can lead to frustration, anger, depression, and feelings of hopelessness. Lastly, while suffering a chronic disease, you aren't the only one suffering. Eventually, everything will spill over onto your friends and family as they try to support you.

RISK FACTORS

Chronic diseases don't just occur; an increase in various risk factors triggers them. While being alive comes with a myriad of risk factors, there are things you're exposed to that can increase the risk factors leading to chronic diseases. Some people are more prone to developing these risk factors than others.

Social and Economic Conditions

Education and income are two enormous driving forces in the development of chronic diseases. People with lower education levels tend to earn less money, leading to poorer healthcare, as they can't afford better. With no treatments, the physical, mental, and emotional toll of the disorder prevents them from trying to achieve a better education.

People with higher education levels tend to have less stress and more access to information about making the correct choices in diet than those with lower education, as they have more money to spend on healthcare and good food.

Children who suffer from chronic diseases tend to fall behind in class as they miss lessons or can't concentrate due to their symptoms. This causes their level of education to be diminished.

In terms of income, it's well known that the higher the poverty level, the higher the rates of diseases (Public Health Agency of Canada, 2023). Many low-paying jobs tend to be labor intensive, meaning there are more physical demands on workers' bodies. However, where others can take time off when ill, these low-paying jobs tend to cut hours or fire those who are constantly ill and replace them with other eager workers. This is why people in low-paying jobs often seem to sacrifice their health, as there isn't the required support to give them the time to get better.

Those on low incomes often can't afford the necessary healthy food, opting to buy the cheapest, regardless of how it can affect their health. They're also less likely to seek medical assistance, instead turning to clinics or emergency rooms as a last resort.

Mental Health

Mental health can be a vicious cycle for chronic diseases, as poor mental health can cause chronic illness, and chronic diseases can trigger poor mental health. Depression, substance abuse, anxiety, trauma, and eating disorders can all play a role in the development of chronic diseases. Depression is often linked to diabetes, heart disease, Alzheimer's disease, and strokes due to the physical and behavioral effects of depression. Someone with depression may be hesitant to seek help, not care about their health, or not take the necessary medication once diagnosed with a chronic disease—leading to increased inflammation, stress hormones, and metabolic changes.

Lifestyle

In some cases, the development of a chronic disease is because of a choice. Poor lifestyle choices—such as drinking excessively, substance abuse, overeating, sedentary lifestyle, and smoking—can increase the risk of chronic diseases.

Drinking excessively increases the chance of developing kidney, liver, and heart disease, and some forms of cancers and type 2 diabetes. Smoking is just as bad, increasing the risk of lung cancer, stroke, and heart disease. Inhaling secondhand smoke increases the risk of developing cancer or asthma, and even babies are at a higher risk of succumbing to sudden infant death.

Other poor lifestyle choices that can boost risks include poor nutrition, inferior sleep quality, and insufficient exercise.

Background

A person's background can make them more susceptible to developing certain genetic chronic diseases. Regarding genetics, in many instances, chronic illnesses are passed down through family lines. However, some people may be affected while others aren't. This is because there is an interaction between the genes responsible for developing chronic disease and the behaviors and environment in which people find themselves. Since most family members tend to have comparable behaviors or live similarly, the risk factors for developing the disorder are higher. This is why it's vital to know your family's medical history to see what you could develop in the future. These conditions can also be linked to gender, age, and race.

Intersectionality and Externalities

Some factors that increase the risk of chronic diseases are beyond your control. These can be intersecting factors such as your race, ability to do necessary tasks, ethnicity, sexuality, and gender.

There are external factors that also play a significant role, such as access to technological advancements and the economic and political situations of your country. Something as simple as missing an opportunity at work can keep you in a dead-end job with a lack of career advancement or upward mobility, which usually leads to a higher income bracket. Political strife can cause an increase in violence, decrease job opportunities, and increase distractions—all leading to elevated stress over situations you have no control over.

Environmental Impact

Since the Industrial Revolution, there has been significantly more pollution in the air. While there has been a conscious decision to lower this, contaminants can still be found in the soil where our food is grown. These toxins wash out into the water we drink, as well as being absorbed into the food we eat, eventually settling in our bodies. Microplastics are already finding their way into our bodies. These tiny particles of plastic can be carriers of environmental toxins that can lead to an increased risk of chronic diseases, such as chronic obstructive pulmonary disease (Lee et al., 2023).

Intermediate Risk Factors

You may already have a condition acting as an intermediate risk factor that can contribute to the development of a chronic disease. Suffering from high blood sugar, high cholesterol, and even high blood pressure can lead to more serious chronic diseases the longer they remain untreated.

Cultural Impact

Each culture is different, but some practices can lead to problems. Specific practices—such as extensive fasting, poor diets, and certain cultural lifestyles—can affect the increased risk factors of chronic diseases. These practices may influence otherwise healthy behavior and even prevent accessibility to proper health care.

How a person looks after their gut health will determine how their health will be impacted. While food plays a major role in the consistency of the microbiome, it isn't the only thing that can upset the delicate balance within the gastrointestinal tract.

Chronic diseases start developing, unseen, for some time before the symptoms appear. With poor lifestyle choices, the environment, genetics, and even culture playing a role in the development of chronic diseases, it can be difficult to pinpoint the reason behind the development of the disease, which can last for months and needs to be managed. There are many risk factors involved in chronic diseases, and most of these can be avoided by living a healthier life. Others, however, are not so avoidable. That isn't a reason to give up on life when diagnosed with a chronic disease, though; there is hope. In the next chapter, we'll look at how it's possible to heal the damage of a chronic disease from the inside by looking at gut health.

CHAPTER FIVE

HEALING FROM THE INSIDE OUT

THE DIGESTIVE SYSTEM AND THE GUT

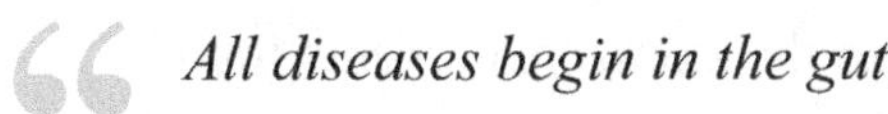

> *All diseases begin in the gut.*
>
> — HIPPOCRATES

In this chapter, we'll look at the roles and functions of the different organs that make up the digestive system and how food, mindfulness, supplements, and nutrition can help fight back against gut disorders.

STEP 1—DISCOVER

Understanding the Digestive Tract and Gut

The digestive tract is a hollow tube that starts at your mouth and ends at your anus. It is made up of several connected and accessory organs. When food is eaten, it is mechanically and chemically metabolized by the digestive tract before the nutrients are absorbed and the waste expelled. Microbes that aid in digestion can be found throughout the digestive tract and have a variety of functions.

Digestive Tract

Each part of the digestive tract plays a crucial role in getting the necessary nutrients:

- **Mouth:** Mechanical digestion takes place with the teeth and tongue mixing the food with saliva to form a bolus, which is then swallowed. Salivary glands secrete amylase, which chemically digests starches.
- **Esophagus:** The esophagus is normally flattened until food is swallowed. It moves food to the stomach via muscular contractions, called peristalsis. The esophageal sphincter, which allows food through to the stomach, prevents food and stomach contents from coming back up.
- **Stomach:** This is the main area for chemical digestion, especially for protein with pepsin enzymes in the stomach acid. Bacteria in this organ are acid-resistant due to the low pH. It contains three types of muscles that help with the breakdown of food and mixing it with digestive juices. The remnants of the food, known as chyme, are slowly drained through a sphincter into the small intestine.
- **Small Intestine:** The small intestine is made up of three parts: the duodenum (for digestion of food), jejunum, and ileum—with the last two sections helping with the absorption of nutrients. Digestive enzymes from the pancreas and liver are added to the duodenum, and peristalsis moves the digesting food further along the small intestine. The small intestine adds water and absorbs it as needed. Bacteria in the small intestines help with carbohydrate digestion,

while fat and protein are further broken down with enzymes. This almost 22-foot-long organ receives semi-solid food and processes it until it's in a mostly liquid state.

- **Large Intestine:** The large intestine is made up of the appendix, cecum, colon, and rectum. It receives the remnants of the mostly digested food from the small intestine and moves it through peristalsis toward the rectum, where mostly waste and some undigested food will be removed. Most of the water absorption is done here, allowing the waste to change from a liquid to a solid. Any remaining food at this stage will have bacteria digesting it further.
- **Rectum:** The final section of the long intestine is where the stool (solid waste) is stored until the body is ready to be rid of it with a bowel movement.
- **Anus:** This is the opening at the end of the rectum that allows for waste removal. It's controlled by two sphincters to prevent incontinence.

Accessory Organs

Accessory organs that work alongside the gastrointestinal tract in the digestive system include:

- **Pancreas:** This organ secretes digestive enzymes through ducts into the small intestine. Enzymes digest fats, carbohydrates, and proteins.
- **Liver:** The liver secretes bile through bile ducts into the small intestine to help digest some vitamins and fats.
- **Gallbladder:** The gallbladder is used to store and concentrate bile. As a meal moves through the small

intestine, the gallbladder squeezes bile through the ducts into the small intestine.

The body cannot do anything with the food we eat if it isn't properly digested, as absorption can only take place with the smaller nutrient compounds.

Each section of the digestive tract has a specific function when it comes to digestion and moving food and drink through the body. The mouth and the stomach do most of the breaking down of food, while the intestines are mostly in charge of absorption, with some enzyme digestion in the duodenum, and the end of the large intestine is for waste removal.

It isn't gravity that moves food, but rather peristalsis. These wave-like muscular contractions slowly move food through the body by contracting at the back of the food and pushing it forward. These contractions not only move the food but also mix in the various digestive enzymes and bacteria, while in some cases helping grind the food.

There are two types of digestion in the digestive tract (NIH, Physiology, Digestion, 202, September 12). The first is mechanical, where the teeth, muscles, and tongue are used to grind, mix, and squeeze the food into easier, manageable pieces. The second, chemical digestion, helps to break the smaller pieces into compounds that make for easy absorption.

Once the food is digested, it's absorbed mostly by the small intestines into the bloodstream through special cells that allow cross-over to the intestinal lining. From here, the various nutrients will go on to be used or stored as needed. The liver oversees storing, processing, and delivering simple sugars, glycerol, amino acids, some vitamins, and many salts. The lymph system will absorb the remaining vitamins and fatty acids.

Digestion should happen spontaneously, thanks to the work of various nerves and hormones. The cells in the lining of the stomach, small intestines, and pancreas all secrete their unique hormones that aid in digestion. Some hormones, such as ghrelin and leptin, play a crucial role in letting you know when you're hungry or full.

Some of the digestive function is controlled by the central nervous system, as many of these nerves are connected to the digestive system. One of the best examples is when you see or smell food and your mouth starts watering, a sign that the body is preparing for a meal. The enteric nervous system—found within the walls of the gastrointestinal tract—has a variety of functions that can help with speeding up or slowing down food movements, controlling peristalsis, and producing digestive juices.

Yet, it isn't just organs and enzymes that help with digestion. Within the digestive tract, billions of microorganisms are working tirelessly. Gut flora, or the microbiome, is an ecosystem that plays a vital role in your health; if something were to happen to them, you would suffer a myriad of problems.

The microbiome not only affects digestion but also affects the intestinal barrier, which keeps food and blood separate. In cases where the microbiome is unbalanced, you can suffer a range of digestive issues, from acid reflux to more serious conditions, such as leaky gut syndrome.

The gut microbiome is made up of a collection of microorganisms that are mostly found in the colon. At any given time, in a healthy individual, there will be over 1,000 different species living in harmony.

You are first exposed to these microbes as early as the womb, as well as when passing through the birth channel and during breastfeeding. As you grow and explore new foods and get exposed to the environment, your body starts diversifying its biome. Each person has a unique microbiome. However, those who live together and share similar diets will have similar microbiomes.

The function of the symbiotic (good) microbiome ranges from digesting fiber by creating short-chain fatty acids, controlling the immune system, affecting brain health (especially moods), and keeping the pathogenic (bad) microbes' numbers at bay. There are a range of benefits associated with having a healthy microbiome. It helps to stimulate a healthy immune system, makes a variety of B vitamins and vitamin K, and protects against pathogenic invaders that may enter your digestive tract with food. The production of short-chain fatty acids (SCFA) helps lower the risk of diseases, colorectal cancer (and others), and a variety of bowel disorders.

When looking at the populations of microorganisms within the microbiome, *richness* is used to describe the size of the population of a specific microorganism, *diversity* describes the number of a variety of microorganisms, and *dysbiosis* is used to describe when the microbiome is unbalanced—usually favoring the pathogenic microorganisms. Low diversity and dysbiosis can cause a variety of issues that vary from metabolic syndrome (leading to type 2 diabetes and obesity) to leaky gut and even irritable bowel syndrome. While a lot of research has gone into discovering how the microbiome affects people, there is still a lot to uncover.

The microbiome isn't just filled with symbiotic microorganisms but also pathogenic microorganisms. This homeostasis can be disturbed by many factors, such as diet, age, genetics, medication, illness, infections, and even injury.

Symbiotic bacteria such as bifidobacteria are required for good digestion, health, and stable emotions. However, when dysbiosis occurs and the pathogenic microorganisms (*Staphylococcus*) take over, there is an increase in risk factors for developing kidney disease, Crohn's disease, ulcerative colitis, and higher cholesterol. This imbalance can also lead to anxiety, depression, autoimmune disorders, and chronic pain. There is even research that shows that the imbalance may affect the genes thought to cause autism (WebMD Editorial Contributors, 2021b).

You have a direct influence on the microbiome, and your actions or inactions can negatively affect it. Here are some ways you could be destroying your microbiome:

- **Consuming too much alcohol:** Consumption of alcohol will cause dysbiosis. However, to what extent will depend on what is consumed. Moderate consumption of red wine can bolster gut bacteria due to the polyphenol content, which helps with lowering blood pressure and cholesterol.
- **Not consuming a wide enough variety of meals:** A variety of meals allows you to get the necessary fiber from fruits, vegetables, and grains. This allows the microbiome to increase.
- **Not consuming prebiotics:** The microbiome needs to be eaten, and there is very little that makes its way to where they are except for indigestible fiber. The microbiome ferments and consumes this food source and makes SCFA.
- **Not doing anything about stress:** As stress increases, there is a decrease in blood flow to the gut, an increase in its sensitivity to inflammation, and the microbiome diversity is disturbed, causing an increase in *Clostridium* (pathogenic) and a decrease in *Lactobacillus* (symbiotic).

- **Not getting enough exercise:** Low to moderate exercise helps improve populations of *Akkermansia* and *Bifidobacterium*, which are health-promoting bacteria.
- **Not getting enough quality sleep:** The gut is affected by circadian rhythm, and if you're not getting enough quality sleep, the gut biome will eventually start to be affected. It only takes a few nights of bad sleep to increase microbes that are associated with decreased fat metabolism, weight gain, type 2 diabetes, and obesity.
- **Smoking:** Smoking not only increases the chance of developing cancer but also causes the most harm of any substance to all organs of the body and is known to increase the risk of inflammatory bowel disease. Quitting smoking will help increase microbiome diversity.
- **Taking too many antibiotics:** Antibiotics are meant to kill bacteria—the bad and, sadly, the good—affecting their richness and diversity. In some cases, taking antibiotics without some probiotics can cause damage to the microbiome that can take years to rectify.

Dysbiosis isn't as simple as pathogenic bacteria outnumbering good bacteria. There are three types of dysbiosis. Type 1 is where there are fewer symbiotic bacteria. Type 2 is when there is an increase in the growth of harmful bacteria. The third type is where there is an overall loss of biodiversity in the good and bad bacteria.

There is no one cause of dysbiosis, and there are likely several factors that come together to cause it. The most well-known reasons for dysbiosis are poor diet (usually the Western diet), medications, excess hygiene, genetics, and stress (physical and psychological). Diets high in sulfur compounds, sugar, and protein and low in fiber can change the balance in the gut, resulting in disrupted mucus membranes and inflammation. Even undergoing chemotherapy for cancer can disrupt the delicate balance of the microbiome.

Some of the signs that you're going through dysbiosis include poor bowel movements (constipation or diarrhea), feeling bloated, mucus in the stool, gas (belching or flatulence), and overall abdominal discomfort. You may even have oral issues such as increased tooth decay and sore or bleeding gums. If not treated, this can worsen health issues such as irritable bowel syndrome, inflammatory bowel disease, and metabolic syndrome.

The effects of dysbiosis on your health can range from mild to serious, depending on how long you ignore it. It can start with chronic fatigue, anxiety, acid reflux, depression, and a range of gastrointestinal issues that will steadily get worse.

Luckily, dysbiosis is curable and can be tailored to your specific needs. All you need to do is change your lifestyle and diet. Avoid alcohol, give up smoking, get some exercise, eat more fiber, and take prebiotics and probiotics. In a severe case of dysbiosis—and only as a last resort—a fecal microbial transplant (FMT) is an option. However, for this to work, the donor needs to be living a similar lifestyle, and the sample needs to be sterile.

However, while dysbiosis may cause a variety of health issues, it can also be indicative of certain disorders developing, like Parkinson's disease. Although it's known that the microbiome plays a role in overall health, it isn't yet completely understood.

Dysbiosis should never be ignored, but how do you know you have dysbiosis and not stomach flu? While some of the symptoms may be similar, there are a few other factors that will play a role in you knowing what you're suffering from:

▷ Developing an upset stomach

- An upset stomach can be dangerous as it can cause dehydration through diarrhea, but it can also cause bloating, gas, food not digesting correctly, and constipation.

▷ Feeling exhausted all the time due to the imbalance that can cause chronic fatigue.

▷ Not getting quality sleep

- The imbalance in the gut can lead to less serotonin being produced, which can affect your mood and sleep.

▷ Suddenly developing an intolerance to some foods

- Different microbes help digest different foods. When not balanced, there's a chance that you can't digest certain foods, leading to more discomfort, bloating, etc.

▷ Unintentional weight fluctuations

- Dysbiosis disrupts fat storage, regulation of blood sugar, and absorption of nutrients. Bacterial overgrowth can also increase weight.

▷ An increase in cravings, specifically sugar

- Too much sugar can cause dysbiosis, and bad microbes crave more, therefore making *you* crave it more frequently.

▷ An increase in skin irritations and headaches

- The skin microbiome can also be affected by dysbiosis in the gut, resulting in psoriasis, eczema, and acne.
- Migraines can become more frequent—especially when you're subjected to nausea and vomiting when suffering a migraine.

▷ Developing autoimmune problems

- Certain pathogenic bacteria can trigger an autoimmune response such as rheumatoid arthritis, thyroid issues, and even type 1 diabetes.

▷ An increased frequency in mood swings

- Imbalances in the gut can lead to inflammation in the nervous system, which results in anxiety and depression.

If you have symptoms such as these, it's a good idea to speak to your doctor to figure out what is wrong and take the correct steps to improve your health.

Leaky Gut Syndrome

While there are people who suffer from leaky gut syndrome, it's not considered a legitimate medical condition but rather a symptom of a larger digestion tract issue. Despite this, a leaky gut can cause many different problems.

In a healthy person, nutrients and water can go through the intestine wall with certain cells at a specific rate known as intestinal permeability. If something occurs in this lining (e.g., illness, inflammation), then nutrients, water, and other undesirable things (partial or undigested food) will pass at a far higher rate than they should. This increased permeability (hyperpermeability) allows more items to pass through the lining than would normally be allowed. The immune system will recognize that foreign objects are passing through the lining and respond, causing inflammation and changes in the gut. It's the continued increase of intestinal permeability and inflammation that will eventually lead to leaky gut syndrome.

While not a cause, leaky gut is often associated with other chronic digestive disorders such as irritable bowel syndrome, celiac disease, and Crohn's disease. Leaky gut may even have a hand in autoimmune diseases, diabetes, fibromyalgia, polycystic ovary syndrome (PCOS), inflammatory bowel diseases, chronic fatigue syndrome, several allergies, and other sensitivities.

As foreign bodies continue to move their way through the intestinal lining into your blood, you may start experiencing symptoms such as chronic constipation or diarrhea, fatigue, confusion, headaches, bloating, widespread inflammation (swollen joints), nutrient deficiencies, and skin issues. Eventually, the gut lining slowly starts to erode, which affects digestion, decreases immunity, and increases sensitivity to pain in the gut. If undergoing radiation therapy, there will be inflammation of the mucus layer.

Some of the causes of leaky gut are thought to be a poor diet, high stress levels, infections or injuries to the digestive tract, chronic inflammation, radiation therapy, diabetes, dysbiosis, autoimmune disorders (lupus), chronic drug misuse, and high consumption of alcohol. Genetics can also play a role.

To treat leaky gut, you will need to change your diet and remove any foods that cause inflammation, replacing them with foods that help lower inflammation and lowering your consumption of processed foods, alcohol, and anything that triggers allergies—while aiming to eat more plant-based foods. You will also have to change your lifestyle, avoid smoking and alcohol, lower your stress levels, get more exercise, improve your quality of sleep, and avoid antibiotics (unless prescribed).

Digestive Tract and Gut Disorders

In 2018, 11% of the US population suffered from some sort of chronic digestive disorder (Avramidou et al., 2018). Those older than 65 made up 35% of them. In 2020, it was discovered that 40% of adults around the world suffered from some form of functional gastrointestinal disorder (FGID) (News in Health, 2019). These are chronic diseases that affect the gut in some way. The symptoms can vary from mild to severe, with some disappearing for years before flare-ups are experienced again. While some disorders are considered acute, most are chronic. There are a variety of disorders that are considered FGIDs, including—but not limited to—reflux, celiac disease, and irritable bowel syndrome.

Gastroesophageal Reflux Disease

This disorder is more often referred to as GERD and starts as simple acid reflux. Acid reflux is when acid from the stomach pushes up into the esophagus, normally after a meal or late at night. It's recognized by a burning sensation in the mid-chest. However, getting acid reflux more than twice a week isn't normal and is then known as GERD.

It's caused when the sphincter above the stomach doesn't close as it should, allowing too much stomach acid to splash up. Occasionally, undigested food can also make its way into the esophagus. The most common symptoms are frequent acid reflux, pain in the chest or upper abdomen, unexplained tooth erosion with a higher rate of cavities, nausea, and bad breath. At night, the symptoms may evolve into a persistent cough, develop or worsen asthma, and even inflame vocal cords.

To ease the symptoms, it may be best to avoid certain drinks and foods. What drinks and foods are person-specific, and some experimenting may be required to find out what sets off your heartburn. Alternatively, the use of antacids and decreasing smoking habits will also help.

Celiac Disease

Celiac disease is caused by an immune response from the body when it comes into contact with the protein *gluten* found in rye, wheat, and barley. While those with gluten sensitivity or intolerance suffer some of the symptoms of celiac disease, it's not as severe.

When someone with celiac disease consumes gluten, their body not only attacks the protein but also attacks the fingerlike protrusions along the intestine walls (villi). When these villi are damaged, it becomes more difficult to absorb nutrients.

Symptoms of celiac disease in children include weight loss, irritability, failure to thrive, abdominal pain, diarrhea or constipation, smelly stool, swollen belly, bloating, and vomiting. Adults share the same symptoms and have fatigue, depression, anemia, seizures, and bone loss. Other symptoms that can occur include mouth ulcers, tingling in hands and feet, a skin rash known as dermatitis herpetiformis, and a decrease in quality sleep.

There is no cure for celiac disease, and it can only be managed with a gluten-free diet. This isn't easy, as many filler ingredients in a variety of packaged foods and medications contain gluten. Careful reading of labels is required, even when you think a food source is safe. While oats are gluten-free, they're often packaged in places where other cereals are. Cross-contamination with gluten can cause problems, so always read labels.

The cause of celiac disease is mostly unknown, but it is speculated that genetics and the diversity of the gut microbiome may play a role in the development of the disorder.

Inflammatory Bowel Disease

Inflammatory bowel diseases are caused when there is chronic inflammation that develops into three different types of inflammatory disorders. These are Crohn's disease, ulcerative colitis, and microscopic colitis. Each disorder is unique in its presentation.

The cause of inflammatory bowel disease is mostly unknown, but there is a possibility that it is caused by the overreaction of the immune system to environmental triggers. The immune system's reaction is inflammation, and if it continues, the chronic inflammation will result in inflammatory bowel diseases. There is also a chance that genetics may play a role in its development, as well as what kind will develop.

The most common symptoms are abdominal pain, gas, bloating, blood or mucus in the stool, a decrease in weight and appetite, and an upset stomach. In rare cases, there could be fatigue, fever, skin rashes and ulcers, and even vision problems.

Crohn's disease can affect the entire digestive tract but is found in the lower end of the ileum, leading into the large intestines. The inflammation caused is in small patches throughout the infected area. Inflammation can affect several layers of the gastrointestinal walls.

The symptoms of Crohn's include rectal bleeding, malnutrition, abdominal pain, fever, diarrhea, abscesses, increased risk of colon cancer, and weight loss. When the symptoms are present, it is known as a flare-up; when the symptoms are minor or non-existent, then it's known as being in remission. However, this is a chronic condition that cannot be cured, only managed—and flare-ups cannot be predicted. The cause is generally genetic.

Ulcerative colitis usually affects the large intestine and the rectum. The inflammation spreads, starting in the rectum and then moving into the large intestine. Only the first layer of the gastrointestinal tract is affected. This disorder has similar symptoms to Crohn's disease but also includes rectal pain, feeling the need to have a bowel movement but struggling through it, fever, fatigue, and diarrhea with pus or blood. The symptoms can develop into life-threatening complications, and there is no cure. Ulcerative colitis also has periods of flare-ups and remission.

The cause of ulcerative colitis is unknown, though it is strongly suspected that the immune system suffers a malfunction, and it starts attacking the body, as well as foreign invaders. There is also strong evidence that genetics plays a role.

Irritable Bowel Syndrome

Irritable bowel syndrome (IBS) is a disorder that will come and go and is mostly triggered by stress. The symptoms are dry or watery stool, bloating, cramping, abdominal pain, and gas. There are rarely any severe problems with this disorder except for a lot of discomfort. It is mostly managed through a change in diet and lifestyle, as certain foods and stress can trigger it.

While the digestive tract doesn't suffer inflammation, it goes through muscle spasms. These spasms can cause the digesting food to be retained for too long, resulting in constipation, or moved through the intestines too quickly, resulting in diarrhea. These spasms can also affect the frequency and appearance of bowel movements. The nerves within the gut lining become extremely sensitive and overreact to pain. During normal digestion, gas bubbles develop in the intestines and rarely bother a healthy person, but someone with IBS will feel discomfort and pain.

This disorder can be caused by infections (like gastroenteritis), stress, and changes in the microbiome. Food that produces a lot of gas—such as cruciferous vegetables—should be avoided—together with caffeine, dairy, alcohol, and even artificial sugars. Diets low in fat and high in fiber are best, but the best diet to try for IBS is the low fermentable oligosaccharides, disaccharides, monosaccharides, and polyols (FODMAP), as this diet doesn't produce the short-chain sugars and fibers that can't be properly digested.

Treating Digestive Tract and Gut Disorders with Foods and Nutrition

It's well-documented that a healthy, well-balanced diet can improve your health, and this is also true for chronic digestive conditions. Most chronic digestive disorders are caused by chronic inflammation, which is caused by the poor Western diet many people consume. The Western diet is known to decrease the total number of microbes in the gut and decrease the number of species in the *Eubacterium* and *Bifidobacterium* groups.

Conditions such as celiac disease have symptoms that can be vastly improved by removing gluten from the diet. Switch to gluten-free grains, such as quinoa and rice, while continuing to eat legumes, a variety of fruits and vegetables, lean proteins, fats, and dairy.

Even GERD can be combated by switching to smaller meals, lowering the consumption of fatty foods and spreading them throughout the day, and avoiding soft or liquid foods in favor of foods higher in fiber.

To help improve your digestion, consider:

- Consuming more whole foods with a variety of fibers. This can boost your gut microbe, which in turn will protect your gastrointestinal lining.
- Eat healthier fats, as this will lower the inflammation in the gut.
- Drink more water to prevent constipation.
- Manage stress levels, as this can affect digestion and cause problems.
- Practice mindful eating and thoroughly chew your food.
- Exercise helps food settle and digest correctly and lowers inflammation in the gut.
- Take the necessary probiotics and prebiotics to bolster the health of your gut microbe.

Try adding a few more plant-based meals in place of highly processed meals. This will help not only improve your gut microbiome but will increase diversity. Keep an eye on the types of fats you consume, as poor fats increase pathogenic bacteria in your gut.

Another point you need to watch with your diet is when you're stressed. Not only does this affect your gut negatively, but it also tricks your brain into reaching for a snack that will give it instant gratification—something high in fat and sugar. Mindfully decide to ignore stressful eating and reach for something healthier.

Food shouldn't just be nutritious; it needs to look and taste good, too. No one wants to just eat a celery stick but add some peanut butter and some pumpkin or sunflower seeds, and you have a delicious snack full of fiber, minerals, and healthy fats. It's not difficult to make the right choice with food; it just takes some time.

With all that said, can food be used to treat digestive disorders, as well as prevent them from occurring in the first place? Yes! All it takes is seven easy steps.

1. Colon Cleanse

Colon cleansing is the act of cleaning waste from the large intestines and has become popular recently, despite the limited scientific research into it. It's believed that the cleanse is supposed to clean up any undigested foods and mucus buildup, which supposedly produce many toxins. These toxins are thought to decrease energy, increase fatigue and weight, and cause headaches.

The benefits of a colon cleanse are said to give a boost to the immune system and mental health, while lowering weight and risk of colon cancer. While there may be benefits, there are also risks that range from mineral imbalances to infections and even possible allergic reactions depending on what is placed in the colon cleanse. In severe cases, this can lead to bowel perforation and even heart failure. Before trying this step, talk to your doctor, as most colon cleanses are aimed at relieving constipation and not improving digestive health. There are many ways to do a colon cleanse:

Drink more water.

- Drinking lukewarm water and eating foods with a high-water content can help with cleaning the colon.

Use a saline flush.

- Drinking saline can help guard against irregularity and constipation.

Increase the fiber content of your meals with more resistant starches.

- Fiber helps move undigested food and waste from the colon. Don't increase too quickly, as this can escalate bloat and gas if your body isn't prepared.

Drink herbal teas.

- Some herbal teas such as aloe vera, psyllium, or marshmallow root have some laxative effects that can ease constipation.
- Use sparingly; talk to your doctor and follow their instructions *to the letter*.

2. Remove Food Triggers from Your Diet

Take your current diet apart, and remove foods and drinks that contain caffeine, artificial sweeteners, high levels of salt and sugar, gluten grains, alcohol, dairy, and all legumes for at least four weeks. This will allow your digestive system to rest and lower inflammation. Experiment with other foods to determine if they cause problems with your digestive tract and remove them if they do. You can even try the low FODMAP diet.

3. Replace and Introduce Recommended Foods

Boost your body's digestion by adding foods that aid in digestion. Foods high in digestive enzymes include bananas, mangoes, pineapples, and even avocados. Not only that, but they contain the prebiotics required by the microbiome.

4. Repopulate With Friendly Bacteria

Don't forget to incorporate probiotics to bolster your existing microbiome. Try fermented foods such as kimchi, sauerkraut, and even miso soup. A drizzle of apple cider vinegar over green veggies gives you the probiotics and prebiotics needed. Don't use antibiotics unless necessary and relieve stress as much as possible.

5. Nourish With Calming Food

Aim to include foods that don't cause inflammation or lower inflammation in your diet. Consider protein- and collagen-rich foods such as bone broth, stews, and casseroles—all easy to digest. You can also add ingredients such as ginger and garlic, snack on berries, or drink green tea for added inflammatory protection.

6. Practice Mindful Eating

Stop wolfing down food! Enjoy preparing smaller meals and chewing thoroughly to savor the moment. The better you chew your food, the better the digestion will be, as the food will be smaller with a larger surface area.

7. Try Intermittent Fasting

Intermittent fasting is when you limit the part of your day in which you're able to consume food. This is meant to lower the number of meals and snacks you can eat. With the body no longer being constantly bombarded by food, it becomes better at digesting what is available. Usually, the body runs on glucose, but when that isn't available, the body switches to the next available resource: the fat reserves. Everyone already fasts when they sleep; those doing intermittent fasting just extend this duration.

There are many benefits to trying intermittent fasting: namely controlling how much is eaten; protecting against chronic diseases such as IBD, some cancers, and heart diseases; and even lowering the risk of type 2 diabetes. Fasting improves memory, blood pressure, and resting heart rate. It can also help lower fasting glucose and insulin, decrease weight, and preserve muscle when losing weight.

Fasting can be done daily, as with the 16:8 technique—or can be reserved for specific days, as seen with the 5:2 technique. To try the 16:8 technique, start by pushing back when you have breakfast. Most people naturally fast for 12 hours a day. Increase the duration of your fast slowly until you reach 16 hours.

Alternatively, you can eat normally for five days of the week and then only eat a single meal on two nonconsecutive days. These single meals shouldn't be more than 500–600 calories. If a single meal is too difficult, you can split the meal into three and spread it throughout the day. This technique can be tough to achieve, so start slowly.

Fasting isn't suggested for anyone pregnant, under 18, who suffers from eating disorders, or who has type 1 diabetes.

STEP 2—ELIMINATE

The next step to healing yourself from within is determining what foods cause inflammation and other problems in your digestive tract. There are a variety of foods that can cause problems for most people but may not necessarily affect you.

The list below includes some common (and some uncommon) poor foods that can affect digestive health:

- **Alcohol:** While alcohol in moderation isn't damaging, heavy drinking can increase the pathogenic microbes and change the balance of the microbiome.
- **Artificial sweeteners:** Consuming too many artificial sweeteners can result in cramps and diarrhea, which increases the risk of pathogenic microbes taking over the gut.
- **Beans and cruciferous vegetables:** These foods contain hard-to-digest sugars for some people, which results in gas and cramping. It's best to soak dried beans for four hours before cooking, and all cruciferous vegetables should be cooked instead of eaten raw.
- **Caffeine:** Caffeine excites the intestines, causing them to work overtime, often leading to diarrhea.
- **Citrus fruit:** If you have a delicate digestive tract, you may find citrus fruits too high in fiber and acidity to digest without discomfort.
- **Dairy:** Avoid if you are lactose intolerant, as this will lead to bloating, gas, and diarrhea.
- **Foods with antibiotics:** Factory-farmed meat comes from animals that are kept in close quarters, resulting in them requiring more antibiotics, which causes their gut microbes

to be affected. Consuming this meat may affect your gut microbes, as well as breeding superbugs.

- **Fried foods:** These negatively affect gut microbes by decreasing diversity, leading to increased inflammation.
- **High fiber:** While fiber is required by the body for healthy digestion, eating too much when the body isn't used to it can result in bloating and gas.
- **High levels of saturated fats:** Eating too many saturated fats increases *Bilophila* microbes, as they deal with the excess bile produced to compensate for too much fat. These microbes can cause an increase in inflammation.
- **Peppermint:** If suffering from heartburn and indigestion, avoid taking peppermint as it has a relaxing effect on the sphincter, keeping the stomach acid back. It's best to take peppermint in capsule form, as it can bypass the stomach and have its benefits delivered to the intestines.
- **Processed foods:** Processed foods are stripped of fiber and full of artificial flavors and preservatives, which can all lead to a myriad of digestive problems.
- **Red meat:** Red meat can cause an increase in bacteria that make compounds that clog arteries.
- **Refined grains:** Refined grains have had their fiber removed, resulting in a simple carbohydrate that's easy to digest but results in glucose spikes and no food being delivered to the gut microbe.
- **Refined sugar:** Sugars such as table sugar, high-fructose corn syrup, and agave sugar decrease healthy gut bacteria, increase inflammation, spike blood sugar, and can even result in cramps, diarrhea, bloating, and gas.
- **Soy:** While soy can be healthy, it has become highly processed, and eating it at high levels can damage your gut

microbes by lowering populations of *Bifidobacteria* and *Lactobacillus*.

- **Spicy foods:** If you're already suffering from indigestion or heartburn, avoid eating spicy foods, as this will worsen symptoms.
- **Spoiled food:** It goes without saying that when in doubt about a food's condition, don't eat it! Microbes such as *E. coli* and *Staphylococcus* can affect food—spoiling it—causing diarrhea, vomiting, and even food poisoning.

If other foods cause you discomfort, remove them from your diet.

STEP 3: NOURISH

Now that you have removed all the foods that cause you discomfort, it's time to nourish your body by adding foods that lower inflammation and help your digestive tract heal.

Below is a list representing some of the most common foods suggested to help improve gut health:

- **Almonds:** This nut is high in fiber, fatty acids, and polyphenols—all of which are great for gut microbes.
- **Avocados:** Not only a low-fructose fruit but one high in fiber, potassium, and good fats—avocados are known to promote a healthy digestive tract.
- **Bananas:** While not a low-fructose fruit, bananas contain fiber inulin, which helps boost the good bacteria in your microbiome.
- **Fermented foods:** Fermented foods are high in probiotics, which will help increase populations and diversity in the

large intestine. Incorporate foods such as kefir, sourdough, kombucha, and yogurt to get more probiotics.

- **Fiber:** Fiber helps prevent glucose spikes, feeds the microbiome, and helps cleanse the colon.
- **Ginger:** Ginger has been used for centuries to deal with a myriad of digestive issues, from bloating to nausea.
- **Leafy greens:** The darker the leafy green, the more essential minerals and vitamins you'll be consuming. They are also high in fiber and low in simple sugars.
- **Lean protein:** Lean protein contains less fat, so it has a lower risk of causing an increase in the bacteria that make compounds that can cause clogging of arteries.
- **Low-fructose fruits:** Not all fruits are equal. Fruits high in fructose can cause bloating and gas. Aim to consume more low-fructose fruits.
- **Olive oil:** One of the best unsaturated fats you can use in your diet, olive oil is high in fatty acids and polyphenols. It helps to lower gut inflammation and ease digestive issues.
- **Plant-based foods:** Plant-based foods aren't only high in fiber; they also contain all the necessary vitamins, minerals, and polyphenols needed for health.
- **Polyphenols:** Polyphenols are molecules that plants use to protect themselves. Consuming polyphenols helps improve beneficial microbes, decreases the pathogenic microbes, and protects the body from inflammation.
- **Seafood:** From fish to shellfish, seafood is high in omega-3 fatty acids that help decrease inflammation while boosting mood and heart health.
- **Whole grains:** Unlike refined grains, whole grains are high in fiber, are complex carbohydrates, and contain omega-3 fatty acids. Consuming whole grains will lower glucose spikes and feed the microbes in the gut.

Not all the foods in this list may bring digestive comfort. If anything in this table causes digestive issues, cut it from your diet.

STEP 4: ENHANCE

Even when consuming better food, your body may still need a helping hand with digestion. Enhancing digestion makes it easier to break down food and absorb nutrients more readily.

Digestive enzymes aim to:

- **Aid digestion:** Some foods are more difficult to break down than others. Digestive supplements can help break down these foods into easily managed parts.
- **Balance the microbiome:** Supplements can be used to introduce beneficial microbes to your existing microbiome, help decrease pathogenic microbes, lower inflammation, and ease other digestive issues.
- **Ensure regularity:** With enhanced digestion comes enhanced waste removal. Supplements help remove waste effectively and in a timely manner, lowering the feelings of bloating and built-up gas.
- **Bring digestive comfort:** The supplements can help ease the discomfort associated with digestion (e.g., bloat, gas, abdominal pain, and so on).

To help enhance digestion, there's a range of digestive health supplements available.

- **Bacteriophages** are organisms that hunt and kill pathogenic bacteria while leaving the beneficial ones alone.

- **Curcumin** is the active ingredient found in turmeric that has anti-inflammatory effects. Be sure to take it with some black pepper so your body can absorb more.
- **Deglycyrrhizinated licorice (DGL)** helps to lower inflammation while increasing mucus production in the gut; this variety of licorice is often used to treat acid reflux and heartburn.
- **Digestive enzymes** can be prescription or over the counter. The supplement should contain all the enzymes required to break down food into smaller, more manageable parts. Some supplements are specifically intended to break down certain foods, while others may offer multiple types of enzymes.
- **L-glutamine** helps support intestinal health by regulating it during stressful times, and it repairs the lining by increasing the growth and survival of the intestinal cells. This supplement can also increase the chance of absorbing necessary nutrients.
- Probiotics and the microbiome are enhanced by eating **prebiotics**. Fiber feeds the microbiome.
- **Probiotic supplements** add to the microbiome populations and diversity and help break down food more effectively. Probiotics also help treat gastrointestinal problems, including relief from IBS and diarrhea.
- **Psyllium** contains a lot of fiber and is known to pull water into the intestines, lowering the chance of constipation and keeping you regular.
- Combined with magnesium, **vitamin C** helps draw water into the gut (as an osmotic agent), which keeps you regular, along with various other benefits.
- **Zinc** helps with keeping the gut permeability where it should be and strengthens the immune system. Together

with L–carnosine and Limosilactobacillus reuteri, zinc can help protect the stomach layer from other bacteria that may weaken it.

Supplements will help enhance your digestion *only* when you're avoiding foods that cause problems with digestion.

STEP 5: BALANCE

Your gut is sometimes referred to as your secondary brain due to the high number of nerves associated with it. This is why, when you're excited or nervous, you can feel your emotions in your stomach. However, this also means that your gut can be influenced by negative emotions and stress.

When undergoing a stressful situation, your brain activates the sympathetic nervous system, which is your fight-or-flight mode. The brain does this by secreting the hormone cortisol—otherwise known as the stress hormone. Your body, faced with what it thinks is a survival situation, starts to concentrate on the parts that will allow it to survive a fight or flight. More energy, nutrients, and blood are sent to the heart, lungs, and limbs—while digestion just grinds to a halt, as it's not needed in a sudden survival situation.

Most of the muscle contractions and secretions associated with digestion grind to a halt. The esophagus goes into spasms, sometimes resulting in vomiting. The level of stomach acid increases and can lead to nausea, and the large intestine increases its motor function—resulting in the urgent feeling of having to have a bowel movement or diarrhea. There is a decrease in blood flow and oxygen to the stomach, which results in cramping, inflammation, and an imbalance in the gut bacteria—which can worsen any digestive orders already present.

Then, once the stressful situation is relieved, the body goes back to being normal in most situations. The sympathetic nervous system needs to be reset by the parasympathetic or its hyperactivity will lead to many problems. The more stress someone is under, the more often this disruption occurs the more difficult it is to recover from. Extended cortisol exposure can decrease the acidity of the stomach, increase the sensitivity of the intestines, and decrease the mucus layer protecting the bowel wall.

Chronic stress will worsen digestive disorders such as Crohn's, peptic ulcers, IBS, GERD, gastritis, and any infections already present in the body, and can cause dysbiosis. The longer the stress continues, the worse the conditions get in those who have them and the higher the risk of developing them in those who don't.

Thankfully, there are many ways to combat stress. New emerging science is proving that mindfulness and meditation may be the key to not only dealing with stress but also creating a microbiome that will help combat future stress.

In an experiment conducted by Sun et al. (2023), blood and stool samples were taken from 37 Tibetan Buddhist monks, along with 19 from the nearby population, to see if a life of meditation affected the microbiome population. The monks were known to have practiced ayurvedic meditation for at least two hours daily for 3–30 years.

It's known that gut microbes are influenced by the gut-brain axis. Meditation allows for the integration of a peaceful mind and body, and thanks to the brain-gut axis, the microbiome can be influenced by behavior and emotions.

When comparing the samples taken from the monks with the other samples, it was noted that the monks had higher concentrations of *Faecalibacterium* and *Megamonas* populations. These microbes are often associated with lower anxiety and depression while boosting heart health and the immune system. They also play a role in well-being and psychosomatic conditions. Not only does meditation affect the gut biome, but it also helps to calm the mind, decreasing cortisol and inflammation and enhancing digestion.

While this study was of a small group of males—who all lived at high altitudes, ate similar meals, took nothing to influence their microbiome, and were the same age with similar blood pressure and heart rates—there is an indication that meditation could influence how the microbiome is influenced through mindfulness.

Stress is known to disrupt the efficiency of the gut barrier and the health of the microbiome. Meditation's soothing effects, it is a great tool to help with decreasing stress-triggered inflammation.

Meditation seeks to target and relieve stress. It activates the parasympathetic nervous system response, the opposite of the fight-or-flight mode. This state is known as the rest-and-digest mode. Allowing your body to enter a relaxed state of meditation will increase the health of the gut barrier, metabolism, and nutrient transportation while decreasing inflammation and helping to relieve symptoms of digestive disorders.

Meditation techniques—such as the loving-kindness technique—help to enhance the vagus nerve as it works with the gut microbiome, increasing gut-brain communication. Even your mood can be affected by meditation. With better diversity in the gut, more serotonin (a neurotransmitter) is produced.

Other studies show that doing yoga and meditation for at least two months is enough to help ease the symptoms of IBS and IBD (Dey, 2015). It isn't your body that can be positively affected by meditation; gene expression can also be affected. Meditation lowers stress and anxiety, affects how genes are expressed (which contributes to the development of IBS and IBD), and lowers inflammation.

Over time, stress-relieving meditation improves the neurotransmitter balance, improves gastrointestinal symptoms, calms chronic inflammation, and improves the health of the gut lining—therefore reducing the risk of developing leaky gut syndrome.

Meditation can also lead to gene expression being changed over time. Relaxation methods affect the pathway controlled by the protein HF-kB (nuclear factor kappa). This protein causes the expression of genes associated with inflammation responses and DNA transcription and, when regulated, can lower inflammation and DNA degeneration.

Meditation also helps lower inflammation by decreasing the concentration of the C-reactive protein (CPR), which is a blood marker associated with inflammation. This isn't the only way inflammation is combated. With a healthier gut microbiome, more short-chain fatty acids are being made, which actively help lower inflammation.

However, meditation is only one way to deal with gut inflammation and needs to be coupled with healthy eating and a healthy lifestyle, free from unnecessary antibiotics. If past traumas are causing stress, these will need to be resolved with a therapist before any healing can occur. Continue to use meditation as a tool but realize that it can only do so much if your poor lifestyle is causing chronic inflammation and stress.

The digestive tract is vital for survival, as without it, there would be no way to absorb the nutrients we need to live a fulfilling life. However, when living an unhealthy lifestyle and eating a poor diet, the gut can become inflamed, affecting the delicate balance in the gut microbiome and resulting in chronic inflammation. This inflammation can increase the risk of many digestive disorders such as Crohn's, IBS, and so on. However, there is time to reverse some risk factors and even soothe symptoms by rebalancing the gut microbiome, lowering stress, and consuming wholesome foods. Lowering inflammation responses is a must, for if they are uncontrolled, there is a chance that the inflammation can spread to other parts of the body, leading to further inflammatory responses and, consequently, more diseases. This will be discussed further in the next chapter.

CHAPTER SIX

INFLAMMATORY RESPONSES AND INFLAMMATION

FRIEND OR FOE? TAMING CHRONIC INFLAMMATION

In this chapter, we'll learn more about how inflammation is vital for your health, but only if controlled. It's possible to control chronic inflammation with supplements, food, nutrition, and mindfulness and possibly reverse any damage already caused.

STEP 1—DISCOVER

Myths About Inflammation

There are many myths surrounding inflammation, such as that having inflammation means you'll have a disease. However, this isn't completely true. Inflammation is an important part of survival, and several myths should be debunked before continuing.

Inflammation isn't a singular condition. Inflammation can affect multiple body parts and organs, as it's a reaction of the cells in the immune system. This is why different types of inflammation can be local or widespread.

Many consider inflammation to be bad when it isn't. The body requires inflammation as it tells us that something is wrong, and the immune system is responding to fix the problem. It's a natural part of the healing process. However, chronic inflammation is usually not good for your health and should be addressed.

Some believe that inflammation will lead to cancer. In some cases, chronic inflammation of the bowel can lead to the development of colorectal cancer. However, no scientific evidence says inflammation can cause other cancers, although it does increase the risk factors for developing cancer. While inflammation can influence the spread of cancer, there is research going into using immunotherapies to help fight the development of cancers.

Inflammation isn't always visible, and if you're not suffering from it, you likely know a few people who are. Inflammation is unavoidable, but it may not always result in a disease developing, as it—alone—isn't the only cause in most cases. Without inflammation, injuries would become infected, fester, and then result in death.

Understanding Inflammatory Diseases

To understand inflammatory diseases, you need to understand what inflammation is. It's the body's process in response to fighting invaders, such as bacteria, viruses, or injuries. Usually, this is a normal process that goes away after a while, but in some cases, the immune system can turn on you and attack the body without there being anything to fight. This is known as an autoimmune disease and will damage your body.

There are two types of inflammation: acute and chronic. Acute inflammation is short-lived—usually a few hours to a few days. This type of inflammation is localized with symptoms that range from redness, warmth, swelling, bruising (associated with trauma), a loss of diminished function (sprained ankle), stiffness, and tenderness or pain. In some cases, the symptoms may mimic flu-like symptoms, including fatigue, headaches, low energy, low appetite, stiff muscles, fever, and chills.

Chronic inflammation is long-lived and can last anywhere from months to years. This is when the inflammation never goes away but continues to exist at persistent, low-grade levels that tend to spread throughout the body. In some cases, there may have been an initial cause for the inflammation, such as a virus, bacteria, or injury, but for some reason, the body never resolved the situation, and the inflammation continued until it became chronic.

Inflammation can be caused by a variety of influences. While invaders and injuries are the main reasons for inflammation to occur, other factors can play a role. Constant exposure (especially allergens), low activity, obesity, diet, sleep disturbances, dysbiosis, and stress are all causes of inflammation. The immune system reacts to these and sends white blood cells to where they are needed. Cells that are damaged will secrete cytokines, which act as an emergency beacon to not only the white blood cells but also the nutrients and hormones that will aid in healing.

Once the white blood cells get to the cells in distress, they secrete antibodies with specific antigens into the surrounding tissues and blood to deal with the problem. This results in an increase of blood flow—causing heat—to the affected area, as well as swelling. The swelling is meant to protect the area and prevent you from injuring it again. However, the swelling also triggers the nerves, and this causes pain. Once the problem is dealt with, the immune system should calm down, but in cases that trigger chronic inflammation, the immune system keeps attacking what it perceives to be the problem. In time, these attacks will extend into the healthy tissue surrounding the initial site, causing inflammation to spread. In some cases, the immune system is hypersensitive to a foreign substance, and every time you interact with it will result in an overreaction by the body to get rid of it.

Good inflammation is when the body reacts to a problem, deals with it, and the flare-up dies down to nothing. Inflammation that isn't dealt with correctly—as with constant exposure to an allergen or stress—that continues to flare up without disappearing is chronic inflammation. This constant inflammation is the reason many chronic diseases develop over time, as well as autoimmune diseases.

Yet, how does the digestive tract influence inflammation and inflammatory disorders? A healthy digestive tract means a healthy immune system that reacts the way that it should, resulting in less risk of chronic inflammation developing. The healthy gut microbiome also plays a role, as some microbes can activate immune T-cells that control or suppress inflammation as needed.

However, when dysbiosis occurs, this disrupts the health of the digestive tract, increasing the level of *inflammatory* cells, while the body can't produce enough *anti-inflammatory* cells. With this abnormal immune response, there is a higher level of inflammation, which increases the risk of inflammatory disorders. While it may start in the gut, as the gut lining weakens, inflammatory cells escape the gut and enter the bloodstream, leaving them free to spread to the rest of the body.

With a lower diversity of gut microbes, pathogenic microbes such as *E. coli* and *Bacteroides fragilis* are free to multiply, triggering an immune response. While the immune system can deal with these pathogens, upon death, they secrete endotoxins, which increase inflammation even more.

Dysbiosis is caused by a range of factors that include—but aren't limited to—smoking, poor diet, chronic stress, high alcohol consumption, misusing pharmaceutical medications, and being exposed to high levels of pollutants.

Inflammatory Diseases

An overload of inflammation can manifest as many diseases as possible, some more serious than others, but all requiring treatment to deal with the flare-ups.

Rheumatoid Arthritis

Rheumatoid arthritis is caused when the body starts attacking the lining (synovium) of the joints. As inflammation occurs, the joints start to swell with the excess liquid until continual flare-ups cause the bone to erode and the joint to become deformed as it shifts out of place. This type of arthritis tends to start in the fingers and toes—where they connect to the hands and feet—before steadily moving upwards to reach the shoulders and hips. Both sides of the body are affected simultaneously.

The first symptoms to be noticed are joints that are stiff in the morning or after a period of inactivity; this is followed by joints that are sensitive, swollen, and warm. In time, fatigue and fevers will develop before a loss of appetite.

About four out of ten people will experience symptoms that affect other parts of their body, such as the skin (rheumatoid nodules), the salivary glands (dry mouth), and inflamed blood vessels, to name some. As the disorder progresses, more internal organs become affected.

The symptoms can vary from mild to severe, with flare-ups coming and going without warning. Genetics is thought to play a small role, while environmental factors—such as an infection caused by a virus or bacteria—are the leading possibility for causing an overreaction in the body to prompt the initial inflammation.

Asthma

When an asthma attack happens, three things occur: the muscles in the airways tighten (causing bronchospasm), the airway lining becomes inflamed and swollen, and more mucus is produced—making the airway more sensitive to asthma triggers. The combination of these three events is what causes an asthma attack, making it difficult to breathe, much less be active or talk. If the inflammation continues for long periods, it can lead to damage in the lungs.

There are different kinds of asthma—generally named after their cause—and the symptoms range from mild to severe. In most cases, the symptoms are mild and tend to stay that way as long as treatment is given quickly. More severe symptoms will occur if the mild symptoms are ignored or as the affected person ages.

The mild symptoms include shortness of breath (which can affect sleep), a tight or painful chest, wheezing when breathing, and coughing (usually early morning or at night). Those with asthma can have all these symptoms or just a few—as it differs from person to person—and each attack can have different symptoms.

Severe symptoms include an increased breathing rate, losing color or turning blue in the face, around the lips, or fingers; having trouble talking, walking, or breathing; and suffering from retractions, where the muscles and skin along the chest contract around the ribs. There is also a chance that, at this stage, medication may not affect the attack, and an ER trip is necessary.

Trying to determine what triggers asthma attacks and causes airway inflammation can be difficult and will require some trial and error. In some cases, exposure to a specific allergen, exercising, and even breathing in cold air can trigger an attack.

Lupus

As with asthma, there are several types of lupus, the most common form being lupus erythematosus. This inflammation disorder is when the body turns on itself and indiscriminately attacks various parts and organs. It's believed that genetics play a central role in the development of lupus, but environmental factors, gender, age, and ethnicity can also play significant roles.

Lupus symptoms vary from person to person, making it difficult to diagnose correctly. It starts with arthritis developing in the small joints in the hands and feet, a butterfly rash that spreads across the nose and cheeks, hair loss, protein in the urine (making it darker than usual), swollen glands, fevers, and even chest pain. Rashes and fever are the symptoms that reoccur the most during a flare-up. Other severe symptoms that may occur include painless but small ulcers in the mouth, increased headaches with the possibility of a stroke, kidney diseases, photosensitivity, and even pericarditis (inflammation of the heart lining).

Though the symptoms tend to start off mild, as the disease progresses, the worse they become—developing into osteoporosis, atherosclerosis, and kidney failure.

Gout

Gout is another type of inflammatory arthritis caused by high uric acid levels in the blood. This is caused when the kidneys can't filter the uric acid out of the body, or the body produces too much. Uric acid comes from the breakdown of purines that come from the digestion of proteins.

Unlike rheumatoid arthritis, gout affects a single joint; in most cases, it's the bunion joint of the large toe. The uric acid crystallizes in the joint, which is what causes the increased inflammation and pain as the white blood cells try to deal with what they see as a foreign invader. When a flare-up occurs, the specific afflicted joint has a lot of pain. However, it's unlikely that this pain will remain there, as over time, other joints further up the leg—and even the fingers, hands, and elbow joints—can become affected. Thanks to the increased uric acid, even the kidneys can be damaged and produce kidney stones.

Genetics and diet play a significant role in the development of gout, and it's seen in men more often than women. Gout is likely to develop more readily in those who have high cholesterol, coronary heart diseases, and dysfunctional kidneys. Foods that can cause flare-ups include alcohol, organ meats, red meats, anything containing high-fructose corn syrup, and shellfish.

How Foods, Nutrition, and Supplements Can Help

The development of chronic inflammation can be influenced by diet. Whole foods high in fiber, whole grains, legumes, fruits, fatty fish (omega-3 fatty acids), and vegetables lower inflammation; other foods such as red meat, processed foods, and refined grains will increase inflammation.

Dietary inflammation is caused by unhealthy blood sugar and fat responses that cause a low level of inflammation. The response to glucose and fat entering the bloodstream is usually handled by various bodily functions. However, those functions can become disrupted when too much glucose and fat are flooding the body, as seen with unhealthy, modern diets. Inflammation will start to occur internally after eating, and symptoms will appear shortly after that. Those affected by dietary inflammation are those with high body mass indexes (BMI), more often men over women, and post-menopausal women over those who aren't.

As established earlier, the gut microbiome is affected by what they are fed. A healthy diet rich in fibers, minerals, vitamins, and polyphenols will produce a rich diversity of microbes that aid health. However, a poor diet will diminish diversity, clearing the way for more pathogenic organisms that hinder health, increase inflammation, and wear down the immune system, making way for inflammatory disorders and various other illnesses.

The best time to change your diet to help your gut microbiome is now because inflammation doesn't get better as you age; it gets worse—and the Western diet is helping no one, no matter how convenient! Foods that are high in antioxidants and anti-inflammatory properties should be on your plate. Diets such as the Mediterranean, Nordic, and Asian are full of whole fruits and vegetables and lean meats (mostly fish) and are enjoyed in smaller portions, while most processed foods are eliminated from the diet.

STEP 2: ELIMINATE

It's always easy to tell someone they need to change their diet, but rarely is what they need to change explained.

The following tips can help you determine what needs to be cut from your diet to help lower inflammation and inflammatory responses:

- **Added sugar:** Consuming sugars releases cytokines, which triggers inflammation. Determining whether something contains sugar isn't always easy, as it has over 50 various names. If something ends in an "-ose," you're likely dealing with a type of sugar.
- **Alcohol:** Alcohol places a lot of strain on a variety of organs throughout the body, which causes inflammation. While elimination is better, one drink or less per day doesn't cause as many problems as excessive drinking.
- **Artificial sweeteners:** The most well-known sweetener is aspartame. While non-nutritional, due to its chemicals, aspartame can cause inflammation as the body sees it as a foreign substance. People already suffering from low-level chronic inflammation should avoid all sweeteners, as they'll worsen the inflammation.
- **Casein:** Those who have dairy sensitivity or are lactose intolerant should avoid any dairy, as casein is its main protein. This protein will cause inflammation in those who are sensitive to dairy.
- **Gluten:** Those who are gluten intolerant or sensitive should avoid eating gluten, as the protein will cause inflammation.

- **Omega-6 fatty acids:** Omega-6 is required by the body but should always be at a lower level than omega-3. High levels of omega-6 lower the effectiveness of lowering inflammation by omega-3. This fatty acid can be found in seed oils (grapeseed, corn, soy, and so on) and vegetable oil and is often found in mayonnaise and salad dressings.
- **Mono-sodium glutamate (MSG):** This chemical is used to enhance the taste of food and is found in various processed foods. Not only can the chemical trigger inflammation, but it can also affect the health of the liver.
- **Processed foods:** Convenience shouldn't have to affect your life expectancy. Processed foods are full of preservatives, artificial colorants, and flavors to make them look and taste better and increase their shelf-life and stability. When the body is hypersensitive, these additives can be seen as invaders, and the body will attack them, causing inflammation.
- **Processed meats:** Processed meats like bacon, sandwich meats, and hot dogs are often cured with nitrates and salts, plus they are high in saturated fats. All three of these substances cause an increased risk of inflammation.
- **Refined carbohydrates:** Anything with the word "white" before it in the name should be avoided—for example, white bread, white rice, and so on. Not only have they been stripped of their fiber, but they have a high glycemic index (GI), which can create advanced glycation end products (AGEs) that cause a spike in inflammation.
- **Trans fats:** This fat is found in fried and fast foods. While there has been a conscious decision to lower the level of trans fats in foods, they are still present. Check the ingredient labels of all packaged foods to see the percentage of trans fats. Avoid food that also has partially

hydrogenated oils. Trans fats are considered far worse than saturated fats.

The first change you should make is to cut away all ready-made meals, which are higher in saturated fats, salt, and sugar.

STEP 3: NOURISH

The Anti-Inflammatory Diet

An anti-inflammatory diet concentrates on consuming whole fruits and vegetables (the fresher, the better), whole grains, and omega-3 fatty acids, to name a few. Ideally, you want to consume highly nutritious foods, high in antioxidants and healthy fats, with as much variety as possible to get all the essential minerals and vitamins. These are foods that are high in antioxidants, which help with the removal of free radicals that are formed through metabolism. A poor diet, smoking, and high levels of stress can increase the number of free radicals in the body. These free radicals damage cells, leading to premature aging and triggering inflammation.

The Mediterranean diet is the most popular of the anti-inflammatory diets. Still, another good diet is the dietary approach to stop hypertension (DASH), which seeks to lower the intake of foods that push up blood pressure. Anti-inflammatory diets are helpful to those who suffer from inflammatory disorders such as rheumatoid arthritis, asthma, lupus, Crohn's disease, and metabolic syndrome.

The Mediterranean diet encourages the consumption of whole grains, lean meats (favoring seafood), fresh fruits and vegetables, low dairy, and moderate volumes of alcohol (usually red wine). The fats in this diet are considered some of the world's healthiest, including avocados, nuts, and extra-virgin olive oil. The diet contains vitamins, minerals, polyphenols, and carotenoids (anti-inflammatory plant pigments) and is low in salt. The diversity of whole foods benefits blood pressure and cholesterol and feeds the gut microbiome, increasing its diversity and health benefits—which is why the diet is heralded as the best way to combat various inflammatory disorders.

The benefit of an anti-inflammatory diet is that it lowers the inflammation already present in your body, even if you're not showing signs of disease yet. The foods in an anti-inflammatory diet do this with their natural antioxidants and polyphenols. Battling the unseen inflammation will improve your physical and emotional health.

If you're not ready to switch to the Mediterranean diet, or you find it too expensive, here's a list of some items you can add to your diet that will benefit your health:

- **Avocados:** They contain fiber, potassium, magnesium, and healthy monounsaturated fats. Avocados contain carotenoids and tocopherols that help to lower the risk of heart disease, cancer, and inflammation.
- **Berries:** High in fiber, vitamins, and minerals, berries are low in carbohydrates. Berries contain anthocyanins, an antioxidant that helps lower inflammation and delays cancer development and its spread.
- **Broccoli:** Broccoli is high in vitamins, nutrients, and minerals. As with all cruciferous vegetables, it helps to lower the risk of cancer and heart diseases and is anti-inflammatory. It contains high levels of sulforaphane, an antioxidant that reduces cytokines and NF-kB that leads to inflammation.

- **Cherries:** Cherries are full of the antioxidants, anthocyanins, and catechins that fight inflammation. Tart cherries have more benefits than sweet ones.
- **Dark chocolate and cocoa:** Cocoa and dark chocolate (70% or more) contain flavanols responsible for lowering inflammation and keeping artery endothelial cells healthy. When choosing cocoa, make sure it is unsweetened.
- **Extra-virgin olive oil (EVOO):** One of the best fats to consume, as it's rich in antioxidants and monounsaturated fats, extra-virgin olive oil will help lower the risk of brain cancer, obesity, heart disease, and more. The antioxidant oleocanthal is responsible for reducing inflammation.
- **Fatty fish:** Considered a lean protein, fatty fish have the long chain eicosapentaenoic (EPA) and docosahexaenoic acid (DHA), which help lower inflammation.
- **Grapes:** Grapes contain anthocyanins and resveratrol that help lower general and heart inflammation, respectively.
- **Green tea:** Considered one of the healthiest drinks, green tea is full of antioxidants with anti-inflammatory properties. It contains epigallocatechin-3-gallate (EGCG) that helps lower cytokine production and damage to the fatty acids within cells.
- **Mushrooms:** Not only low in calories but also high in selenium, copper, and the vitamin B complex, mushrooms contain phenols and antioxidants that contribute to lowering inflammation.
- **Peppers:** Sweet and hot peppers are high in vitamin C and have strong anti-inflammatory properties, which help lower inflammation from chronic diseases. They contain sinapic and ferulic acid, which also helps with lower inflammation and healthier aging.

- **Tomatoes:** Tomatoes are high in vitamin C, potassium, and carotenoid lycopene, an antioxidant that lowers the pro-inflammatory compounds associated with some cancers.
- **Turmeric:** This spice contains curcumin, a powerful anti-inflammatory known to lower C-reactive protein (CPR) markers associated with inflammation. Turmeric needs to be taken with piperine to absorb the curcumin better.

Remember, the higher the variety of fruits and vegetables you consume, the more benefits you'll receive.

STEP 4: ENHANCE

There are supplements that can help with lowering inflammation. In some cases, these are extracts of foods that can be added to your diet. Be sure to speak to your doctor before adding these to your lifestyle changes.

Bromelain is an enzyme found in pineapple and is an astringent. It's a potent anti-inflammatory that's often thought to be better than nonsteroidal anti-inflammatory drugs, with fewer side effects. It has been used to lower the inflammation associated with wisdom teeth removal.

Curcumin extracts are available, or turmeric can be added to food. Use black pepper to have the piperine needed for absorption. It helps lower the inflammation associated with rheumatoid arthritis and osteoarthritis.

Fish oil is high in omega-3 fatty acids converted to alpha-linolenic acid, an essential fatty acid. The fatty acid DHA is known to increase gut health, fight cytokines, and help lessen muscle degeneration after exercise. If you are a vegetarian or vegan, you can swap fish oil for canola oil, which contains omega-3 and vitamin E. If you are taking blood thinners or are immunocompromised, speak to your doctor before supplementing.

The antioxidant garlic helps strengthen the immune system and improves inflammatory markers IL-6 and tumor necrosis factor-alpha (TNF-α).

Ginger contains the antioxidants gingerol and zingerone, which help lower inflammation by lowering CRP markers and interleukin-6 (IL-6) and helping control blood sugar.

Green tea extract is more potent than the drink, with higher levels of EGCG. Be wary that some green tea extracts may have caffeine, so be sure only to take an extract that states it's caffeine free.

Extracted from grapes, resveratrol is an antioxidant that helps improve ulcerative colitis symptoms, improves quality of life, and lowers inflammation, triglycerides, and blood sugar. Resveratrol also offers protection against liver disease.

Spirulina is algae containing strong antioxidants that help fight inflammation, improve the immune system, and support healthy aging. Be wary if you're allergic to shellfish, as this could cause a reaction. There is also a chance of a response if you have autoimmune conditions.

Vitamin C boosts the immune system while lowering inflammation and wear and tear on cells. However, please don't take too much, as it can lead to diarrhea.

Vitamin D has strong anti-inflammatory properties and helps to boost overall health. A low vitamin D level is often associated with higher inflammation than average. Limit the intake of this vitamin, as being fat soluble, it can be stored—leading to toxicity if too much is consumed.

Many of these supplements have already been proven to boost the gut microbes, which in turn give an extra boost to lowering inflammation through various means.

STEP 5: BALANCE

While your diet does play a vital role in your health and can diminish inflammation, it isn't the only factor. The communication between the central nervous system and the systemic immune system also controls inflammatory responses. Remember that your gut makes up a large portion of your immune system, which is connected to the central n5ervous system.

When suffering from psychological or physiological stress, your body activates several pathways that promote inflammation. This, in turn, triggers the need to overeat when not hungry—generally on unhealthy meals. This poor eating pattern causes more stress, such as worrying about your health, increasing inflammatory foods, and so on—which continues with wanting to eat more unhealthy foods, causing a vicious cycle. This results in increasing weight, metabolic disorders, and an increased risk of developing other inflammatory diseases.

Because these two systems communicate the way they do, just changing your diet or behavior isn't enough. They need to be changed simultaneously. Having a good diet, making good lifestyle choices, and dealing with stress meaningfully is vital.

Mindfulness—meditation, mindful eating, tai chi, and so on—is often used to help manage stress. It can help calm and uplift you with positive emotions and helps lower your body's response to anxiety or stress, leading to less inflammation. It can also help change the brain's structure, helping it to be less likely to overreact to adverse situations and allowing you to worry less and have lower stress. It's also believed that mindfulness can alter your DNA so that your body slows down the activity of some of the genes associated with inflammation.

Meditation helps the brain establish a better connection between its executive attention network, which allows you to make decisions, plan, and pay attention, and the default mode network, which allows your mind to wander and have internal reflections. Thanks to this, there is a decrease in CPR and IL-6 markers, but not significantly in everyone, as science has mixed results.

In a study completed by Villalba et al. (2019), it was determined that mindfulness is most beneficial to those over 45 and who have a higher BMI than others with lower than 5average inflammation, as it's these people who are more vulnerable to stress. Does this mean mindfulness won't be effective for you if you fall outside of these categories? Not at all!

When stressed, the body releases cortisol, which prepares the immune system to take on a potential threat. During this time, cytokines are being made to help attack potential invaders. However, cytokines are—in themselves—inflammatory. With chronic stress, inflammation becomes chronic, increasing the risk of inflammatory disorders such as Alzheimer's disease, arthritis, or heart disease from developing.

Cortisol and stress can be managed and decreased through meditation, making you calmer. Mindfulness helps to control inflammation by controlling what causes it, helping to buffer the adverse outcomes of stress.

Being mindful doesn't require much time. You don't need to be a Tibetan monk who meditates for multiple hours a week. It takes as little as ten minutes a day of regular mindfulness to start improving stress levels. Start with a few minutes daily and steadily build up to ten minutes or more if you're comfortable. While some people feel meditation is the best way to practice mindfulness, there are many other ways to be mindful, such as taking a slow walk, focusing on gratitude, or even silently sitting in prayer.

While inflammation is often viewed as negative, it is necessary to keep you healthy and capable of healing. However, when inflammation continues uncontrolled for too long, it can cause many problems, such as the body attacking itself because it has become hypersensitive to environmental factors and developing inflammatory diseases. To help reduce inflammation, you can take positive steps by changing your diet, removing yourself from harmful environmental factors (smoke, pollutants, and so on), and living a more active lifestyle to lose excess weight. Even taking a few minutes to yourself daily can help lower cortisol production and manage stress levels through mindfulness. In the next chapter, we'll look at how the immune system can be boosted to tackle autoimmune diseases by looking at the links between the digestive tract, the gut, and inflammation.

CHAPTER SEVEN
EMPOWERING THE IMMUNE SYSTEM
THE LINK BETWEEN DIGESTIVE TRACT, GUT, INFLAMMATION, AND AUTOIMMUNE DISEASES

This chapter will explore how autoimmune diseases are linked to inflammation and the digestive tract. We'll also cover the use of mindfulness, food, nutrition, and supplements in treating and possibly reversing the damage.

STEP 1: DISCOVER

Western medicine cannot cure autoimmune diseases but relies on corticosteroids and nonsteroidal anti-inflammatory drugs to help prevent the body from turning on itself. However, is this the only way, and can this be maintained in the long run?

The Immune System

The immune system is a network of organs (internal and external), cells, antibodies, and more—that protect you from foreign invaders, such as viruses and bacteria. Its job is to fight foreign invaders, learn to recognize and destroy harmful intruders, and even fight disease-causing changes in the body (cancer cells).

There are two parts to the immune system: the one you're born with and the one you acquire. The innate immune system is a nonspecific immune system that all babies are born with. It's mostly made up of physical barriers such as the lining of the skin; the gastrointestinal, genitourinary, and respiratory tracts; and the cornea. This is genetically inherited. The adaptive or acquired immune system will slowly develop over time as the baby is exposed to more foreign invaders. Exposure to these intruders allows the body to have many antibodies, which protect the body at the time of the attack and in the future when the foreign invader returns. After a time, similar infections won't result in serious illness.

The immune system consists of the following components:

- **Bone marrow:** The bone marrow is responsible for creating red blood cells, some white blood cells, plasma cells, and a variety of others. It releases billions of these cells into the bloodstream daily.
- **First line of defense:** The skin is a waterproof organ that produces oils and other protective immune system cells. The mucus membranes make sticky mucus that not only lubricates and moistens the area but also traps invaders. Areas covered in cilia (little hairs) will move invaders out. These first defense structures aim to prevent and destroy foreign invaders before they get deeper into the body. Other defenses come from bodily fluids, such as tears, skin oil, saliva, and so on, which are antibacterial and contain enzymes that lower the risk of infection.
- **Lymph nodes:** These glands are part of the lymphatic system and contain immune cells that recognize invaders

and send specific white blood cells as needed. The glands also help filter and destroy invaders. Lymph nodes are found throughout the body and become swollen when fighting an infection.

- **Spleen:** This organ filters blood cleans it of old and nonfunctional red blood cells and stores white blood cells.
- **Stomach and bowel:** The stomach acid kills most of the bacteria swallowed, while beneficial gut microbes will deal with those that reach the intestines.
- **Thymus:** The thymus rests behind the breastbone in the upper torso and is responsible for maturing T-cells (T-lymphocytes). These cells are responsible for recognizing and remembering foreign invaders, making the response time to deal with the invader at a later stage much quicker.
- **Tonsils and adenoids:** These are the first organs in the line of defense for the internal immune system, as they're in the throat and nasal passages. Immune cells in these organs produce antibodies against invaders that cause lung and throat infections.
- **White blood cells:** Also known as lymphocytes, there are many different kinds with specific jobs, such as hunting, attacking, and destroying foreign invaders. Some cells circulate freely through the body, while others are produced as needed. These cells can also communicate with other cells that help defend the body.

One of the side effects of the immune system working is the presence of a fever. The increased temperature can kill certain bacteria and trigger the body's ability to self-repair. However, a fever that is too high can cause more problems.

Thanks to your immune system, you can remain primarily healthy despite being bombarded with invaders like bacteria, viruses, and pollen. Occasionally, the immune system doesn't work the way it should. Instead of *defending* your body, it ceases to function as it should or turns on you by *attacking* the body, resulting in allergic reactions to things you aren't allergic to or autoimmune diseases.

There are a variety of conditions and disorders that can cause the immune system to malfunction and attack healthy cells. While in some cases, genetics and environmental factors are to blame, some medications can also be thought to trigger the disorders. Cancer, infections, sepsis, and other autoimmune diseases can also lead to other autoimmune conditions developing.

Understanding Autoimmunity

With a normal immune system, antibodies are created to match the antigens on foreign invaders, which helps them recognize and deal with them. However, when an immune system malfunctions, the antibodies don't recognize the body's cells as autoantigens (self-antigens). Unable to recognize friends from foes, the immune system mounts a defense against the autoantigens with autoantibodies, which are designed to attack autoantigens. While this does occur occasionally, the body has a certain tolerance for this, but only up to a point; once this point is exceeded, an autoimmune response occurs, and various disorders can develop. An autoimmune disease follows when there is damage to specific tissue types (organs, joints, and so on) or the whole body is affected. Some of the autoimmune diseases that exist include psoriasis, Graves' disease, Hashimoto's thyroiditis, type 1 diabetes, and many more.

One of the most common factors in the development of autoimmune disease is gender, as biological females 15–44 are more likely to be affected. Other common causes are genetics, environmental factors, ethnicity, nutrition, and smoking. Even health conditions, such as obesity, can play a role. Certain medications can trigger lupus. However, the truth is that the exact reason is unknown.

Common symptoms of an autoimmune disorder are rashes, hair loss, muscle aches, fatigue, low-grade and recurring fevers, and swollen glands. All these symptoms can easily be dismissed as an immune response to the common cold, which makes correctly identifying an autoimmune disorder difficult. Other symptoms that can be experienced include digestive issues, abdominal pain, and trouble concentrating. Even with these added symptoms, they are still like many other disorders, and it can take several flare-ups and remissions before an autoimmune disease is diagnosed correctly.

Inflammation is considered one of the many causes of an autoimmune response. The body believes something is wrong and tries to deal with it, causing an inflammatory reaction. A malfunctioning immune system will continue to attack the affected area, even if the original cause of the response is long gone, leading to more inflammation that becomes chronic and can even spread to surrounding regions.

One of the many factors science is looking at to understand why an immune system would malfunction is the gut microbiome. It's believed that the gut microbiome influences the rising occurrence of autoimmune diseases. We already know the gut microbiome's influence on inflammation, so it's not a far stretch that it could also play a role in autoimmune disorders.

Gut dysbiosis influences health, as much of the immune system is found along the gut. The gut and its microbiome are heavily affected by diet. A diet high in salt causes a decrease in the *Lactobacillus* bacteria, which produces metabolites associated with suppressing pro-inflammatory cells, leading to an increase in inflammation. Any adverse change to the gut microbiome changes the immune system. One of these changes is the development of leaky gut syndrome. Not only does this problem cause a diminished capacity to absorb crucial nutrients, but it also causes larger-than-normal gaps in the intestinal lining that can unintentionally allow intestinal contents to enter the bloodstream. This leads to foreign particles being targeted by the immune system, creating inflammation. Yet, it isn't just inflammation that is the problem. Undigested food particles can become labeled as invaders—meaning, if you eat these foods later, you may have an allergic reaction due to your immune system thinking it's an intruder. Other cells that come from the intestines are also targeted similarly, leading to them being attacked in other parts of the body, regardless of them being beneficial or pathogenic. The inflammation will continue to spread, causing a low-level inflammation that eventually becomes chronic. Constant leaking of intestinal contents will increase inflammation, food sensitivities, indigestion, and abdominal pain—which, in turn, will continue to erode the intestinal lining, causing more leakage.

Irritable bowel disorders and Crohn's disease are already caused by immune dysfunction due to gut microbes. This leads to the theory that inflammation caused by gut microbiome problems leads to inflammatory issues and autoimmune disorders. Constant inflammation also increases the immune system's sensitivity, making it more prone to overreact to anything happening in the body. This enforces the theory that a leaking gut can cause inflammation.

It isn't just gut dysbiosis that can cause a problem with the immune system. Didelot et al. (2016) found within-host evolution of the bacteria *Enterococcus gallinarum* in a mouse study. This bacterium is linked to diseases such as meningitis, endocarditis, and, in severe cases, sepsis; it is generally found within the intestines, where it's kept under control by the beneficial microbes. The study found that *E. gallinarum* underwent mutation in its DNA, allowing it to live within the intestinal wall and eventually break free to settle in the liver and lymph nodes. This invasion wasn't noticed at first, but once it was, the immune system of the mice responded with inflammation to deal with it. It's believed that because the evolution occurred within the mice's body, it took their immune system longer to recognize the threat, allowing it to spread further and cause widespread inflammation.

This study was performed on mice, and how this translates to humans is still being studied. However, the study outcome provided scientists with a better understanding of how the microbiome can influence an immune response (Didelot et al., 2016).

While this study was with an animal model, other human studies show a connection between the balance of the microbiome, a leaking gut, and the start or worsening of autoimmune conditions (Christovich & Luo, 2022).

Autoimmune Diseases and Disorders

There are over 80 different kinds of autoimmune disease. Most of these are incurable, while others require lifelong treatments.

Multiple Sclerosis

Multiple sclerosis (MS) occurs when the immune system starts to attack the myelin sheath around the nerves, affecting the brain's ability to communicate with the central nervous system and the rest of the body. These autoimmune diseases cause is unknown but linked to genetics and environmental factors. There is no cure, but treatments can help recovery after a flare-up, speed up that recovery, and help manage the symptoms.

The symptoms are highly variable depending on which nerves are attacked. One of the most common symptoms is that a person starts struggling to walk or loses the ability to walk after some time. Other symptoms include numbness or weakness in limbs (affecting one side and then the other), electric-like shocks when bending the head forward, low coordination, partial or complete blindness (first one eye, and then the other), vertigo, fatigue, tingling, cognitive problems, and even slurred speech. There may even be pain or muscle spasms.

Flare-ups can repeat the same symptoms or develop new ones over time. In some cases, it can be months or years between flare-ups. Roughly 20–40% of MS patients suffer from relapse-remitting MS, with a steady progression of symptoms that may be with or without remission, also known as secondary progressive MS (Mayo Clinic Staff, 2022f).

Multiple sclerosis will eventually affect movement, sensation, bowel and bladder control, coordination, and sight as the nerve fibers start to become damaged. While not fatal, complications such as trouble swallowing, or infections can arise that can be deadly.

Type 1 Diabetes Mellitus

In type 1 diabetes, the immune system turns on the insulin-making beta cells of the pancreas. As the body can no longer produce insulin, blood sugar can't be controlled, causing high glucose levels in the blood while the cells starve. The increased blood sugar will cause damage to cells, diabetic ketoacidosis, dehydration, and weight loss. It's believed that type 1 diabetes is caused by either genetics or a virus that causes the body to attack the pancreas.

The initial symptoms include increased hunger (despite eating), increased thirst, frequent urination, and frequent infections of the skin, urinary tract, or within the vagina. If the blood sugar levels aren't controlled, the symptoms will worsen, including fruity breath, shaking accompanied by confusion, rapid breathing, and even a loss of consciousness. Someone with type 1 diabetes will require injectable insulin to survive.

Psoriasis

Psoriasis is a rash that develops itchy, scaly patches, usually at joints, such as knees and elbows, or along the trunk or scalp. There is no cure, and the condition can become painful, especially when the skin dries out and cracks, introducing new infections and decreasing sleep quality and concentration. A cause of psoriasis is an increase of T-cells below the skin, causing the body to attack the skin. Another probable cause is that skin cells are growing faster than they should.

As with other autoimmune disorders, Psoriasis has flare-ups and remissions but can be triggered by many factors. When suffering from psoriasis, it's important to avoid injuring the affected sites, as in cuts or burns, or this can trigger the rash to reoccur. Other triggers include fungus infections, the weather, smoking, excessive alcohol consumption, and certain medications. Different types of psoriasis affect different parts of the body.

Hashimoto's Disease

Also known as Hashimoto's thyroiditis, this autoimmune disorder is caused by the body attacking the thyroid gland, causing hypothyroidism. The thyroid can take years of decline before symptoms are noted. Due to less thyroid hormone, symptoms such as muscle weakness, increased sensitivity to cold, swollen thyroid (goiter), increased tiredness, depression, hair loss, brittle nails, and constipation will occur more frequently.

There is no cure, and those with Hashimoto's will be on thyroid replacement for the rest of their life. This disease is caused by genetics, environmental triggers like high radiation, and even other autoimmune disorders such as lupus.

Graves' Disease

Graves' disease is similar to Hashimoto's, as the immune system attacks the thyroid. However, instead of decreasing the thyroid hormone, the thyroid produces too much. The cause of this is that when antibodies attack the thyroid, there is a specific type of antibody—the thyrotropin receptor antibody (TRAb)—that starts to regulate the production of thyroid hormone instead of the pituitary gland. It is unknown why this occurs, but it's likely due to genetics and environmental factors.

The symptoms include increased anxiety, changes to the menstrual cycle or erectile dysfunction, low libido, goiter, bulging eyes, sleep disturbances, and heart palpitations. The only way to prevent hyperthyroidism is to remove the thyroid and then use hormone replacement therapy to replace the thyroid hormone.

How Foods, Nutrition, and Supplements Can Help

We still don't really understand how autoimmune diseases develop, with genetics and environmental factors being cited as the leading causes in most cases. However, diet is another factor that may trigger or soothe autoimmune symptoms. A good diet, full of whole foods, good proteins, healthy fats, and low in processed food, lowers inflammation, while a poor diet promotes it. While not all autoimmune diseases are caused by inflammation, many have it. A healthy diet, physical activity, and the correct supplementation of specific vitamins (such as vitamin D) lead to less inflammation and lower the risk of various autoimmune diseases, such as type 1 diabetes and MS.

A bad diet is also known to cause poor gut health, leading to dysbiosis, increased intestinal permeability, and, eventually, a leaky gut. When food particles escape into the body, they may be falsely recognized as foreign bodies, leading to the theory of molecular mimicry. The immune system attacks these molecules and anything else similar; if that's a specific cell or organ, it'll be attacked as if it were an invader, causing inflammation and other problems.

Enjoying a healthier diet promotes a healthier gut, and some foods contribute to lowering inflammation by preventing pro-inflammatory cells from causing inflammation. The increase in autoimmune diseases corresponds with more people having access to the Western diet, which is high in processed foods (Wood, 2022). A change in diet may not cure autoimmune diseases, but it'll lower the symptoms, decrease flare-ups, and improve quality of life.

What you eat is important. Eating foods high in fat, sugar, and salt while having low activity will lead to obesity. Those with obesity develop white adipose tissue that stores energy and releases many pro-inflammatory chemicals (e.g., IL-6, CRP, and so on) and is now considered an endocrine system and not just a layer of fat.

STEP 2: ELIMINATE

Various foods can trigger an immune response through intestinal inflammation or dysbiosis, leading to autoimmune diseases.

- **Caffeine and alcohol** can affect our immune system. Alcohol can increase the permeability of the intestine, leading to a leaky gut. While not true for everyone, there is a chance that coffee may trigger food intolerances and increase inflammation. If trying the autoimmune protocol diet, you may only need to remove caffeine temporarily.

- Many **dairy products** are high in fat, which triggers inflammation.
- **Eggs** are high in cholesterol and fat and have pro-inflammatory properties. They also contain proteins that can appear as harmful foreign substances that leak through the gut.
- Known to increase gut permeability, **food additives** can lead to a leaky gut.
- **Gluten-containing grains** are high in the plant compound lectin, which can increase the permeability of the intestine. These types of grains should be avoided if you're sensitive or intolerant.
- **Legumes** contain lectin, which can increase intestinal permeability.
- **Nightshade vegetables** such as potatoes, tomatoes, peppers, and eggplants all contain alkaloids, such as glycoalkaloids, that can irritate the gut. They also contain lectins. An irritated gut can lead to inflammation and can start to leak.
- Many people are sensitive to **nuts and seeds** due to their allergen-producing effects. It's wise to avoid spices made from nuts and grains.
- **Refined oils** made from nuts and seeds should be avoided as they cause an increase in inflammation and can have an allergen-producing effect.
- **Refined sugars** increase inflammatory cell production, and the increased blood sugar will also cause inflammation after some time.

- You may also have to be wary of adding extra **vitamin C** and beta-carotene or supplementing with ginseng or echinacea to improve your immune system when suffering from autoimmune diseases. This may cause your immune system to ramp up the symptoms of your autoimmune disease.

STEP 3: NOURISH

The Autoimmune Protocol Diet

The autoimmune protocol (AIP) diet is an elimination diet aiming to discover what is causing autoimmune symptoms. Once various food types have been eliminated, the symptoms of autoimmune disease will start to improve. This allows you to identify what food is causing the multiple signs, which can then be eliminated from the diet permanently. This will enable you to tailor your diet to your body's responses.

The diet is done in two phases: the elimination phase and the reintroduction phase. During the elimination phase, foods that should be avoided should be cut from the diet and not consumed until all the autoimmune symptoms are gone. You may have to cut nonsteroidal anti-inflammatory drugs (NSAIDs) from your life, as you want to be sure you're not lowering your inflammation artificially.

After the improvement, you can reintroduce the foods you have previously cut out. Do this *one* at a time and slowly:

1. Choose some from the *avoid eating* table and consume no more than one tablespoon full. Wait for 15 minutes to see if there is a reaction.

   a. If a reaction occurs, end the testing and wait for the symptoms to subside to try a different food. Continue to the next step if there is no reaction.

2. Try a more significant portion, one and a half tablespoons of the food you're testing and wait two to three minutes for possible symptoms.

   a. If a reaction occurs, end the test. Allow the symptoms to subside before choosing a new food to try. Move on to the next step if you do not react.

3. Eat a regular portion of the food chosen, then avoid it for the next five to six days and introduce no new food at this time.

   a. If there are no reactions within a week, this food is safe to return to your diet. Move on to trying another food item off the list and repeat all the steps above.

When deciding on testing different foods, ensure you aren't ill, stressed, or lacking in sleep—as this will affect the amount of inflammation you experience. When testing foods with various contents, such as the lactose in dairy, start with foods that have less. You may find you can stomach yogurt but not milk, meaning you can still enjoy dairy, just not all kinds.

Avoid eating highly processed commercially produced industrial foods made with refined and bleached flour, processed sugars, seed cooking oils, and salts as food preservatives for a longer shelf-life. These heavily marketed foods are mass produced, distributed, and manufactured to be extremely cost-effective to appeal to the masses. They are laden with highly processed white wheat flour and added sugars, including, but not limited to, alcohol sugar and many other types of sugars that are used and sold under disguised names. There are at least 61 different names for sugar listed on food labels. These include common names, such as sucrose, high-fructose corn syrup, barley malt, dextrose, maltose, and rice syrup, among others, which are used in commercially produced supermarket foods: such as sweet things like cookies, cakes, bottled and powdered sodas, and fruit juices; as well as many savory foods, such as bread, pasta sauces, bottled and powdered coffee, dairy, eggs, food additives, grains, legumes, nightshades, nuts and seeds.

Enjoy eating bone broth, fermented foods, fruits, herbs, spices, low-processed meat, low-processed vegetable oils, black and green tea, sweet potatoes and yams, vegetables, vinegar, and limited amounts of natural plant-based sweeteners like honey.

The AIP diet is said to help, as the foods removed from the diet are often associated with increased intestinal permeability and inflammation. This diet has already been used to help lower the inflammation and symptoms of inflammatory bowel disease (Konijeti et al., 2017) and modify the inflammatory pathways in ulcerative colitis to prevent triggering inflammation (Chandrasekaran et al., 2019).

However, there are some dangers associated with the AIP diet. The first is that, while it is an elimination diet, it is also a restrictive diet—meaning that if you're on it for too long, there's a chance that nutritional deficiencies will develop. It's also a difficult diet to adhere to, and each slipup causes negative immune responses over time.

STEP 4: ENHANCE

There are a few supplements you can take to help support the fight against autoimmune disorders and their symptoms:

- **Curcumin:** Highly anti-inflammatory, curcumin helps suppress two different pro-inflammatory metabolic pathways. It supports a healthy immune system.
- **Fish oil:** Fish oil helps to regulate inflammation genes while lowering the risk of autoimmune diseases developing due to its omega-3 fatty acids combating inflammation. The omega-3 fatty acids help reduce intestinal permeability and vascular inflammation, which aids in protecting the heart. Most of the benefits of fish oil are noted in combination with vitamins D and A.
- **Glutathione:** A potent antioxidant, glutathione helps bind and eliminate various toxins and free radicals. While produced naturally in the body, daily stresses can diminish it, leading to more inflammation due to higher oxidation levels and free radicals. The immune system requires glutathione to function optimally.
- **Probiotics:** Increasing the health of the gut microbiome will help lower gut permeability and inflammation.
- **Resveratrol:** Highly anti-inflammatory, resveratrol helps you age more healthily and supports the white blood cells in their activity while lowering autoantibody production. It helps to inhibit cytokines and support heart health, as many people with autoimmune disorders have heart conditions.
- **Vitamin D:** A lack of vitamin D is known to cause various problems, so adding more to your diet will help support the immune system while improving overall health along with the health of bones and skin. Vitamin D can help regulate

genes involved in inflammation, altering how the immune system responds and lowering the risk of autoimmune disease from developing.

It's vital to remember that taking supplements now and again won't change your health for the better. This isn't an instant fix. Speak to your healthcare professional about what would best suit you.

Also, be wary of using just any supplementation when you already have an autoimmune disease. Supplements such as echinacea, spirulina, chlorella, and alfalfa (lucerne) can increase cytokines and inflammation, especially in autoimmune skin diseases or skin symptom flare-ups, such as lupus erythematosus.

STEP 5: BALANCE

It's already known that stress causes inflammation, but is there a link between stress and autoimmune diseases? When a person suffers a specific stressful event, it can lead to a stress-related disorder—such as post-traumatic stress disorder (PTSD)—resulting in maladaptive behaviors in response to further stressful situations. It's these stress-related disorders that lead to an increased risk of developing one or multiple autoimmune disorders compared to those without a stress-related disorder. Continued stress coupled with poor lifestyle choices like smoking, inactivity, and so on can exacerbate the symptoms.

There are various degrees of stress. Some are caused by excitement, such as your wedding day, while others are more distressed. It's the distressing stress that causes the increased inflammation seen in those who suffer from chronic stress. It would only take a significantly bad day for chronic stress to develop into a stress-related disorder. Psychological stress is already known to be a risk factor in the development of Graves' disease and rheumatoid arthritis (Mymee, 2022). The type of stress and its duration affect the development of inflammation-driven autoimmune diseases.

Numerous studies have indicated that psychological and physical stresses affect the immune system and how it functions, as seen in animal and human models (Stojanovich & Marisavljevich, 2008). Many people in these studies (up to 80%) stated that they suffered uncommonly high stressful situations before noting the onset of autoimmune symptoms. Sadly, the development of autoimmune diseases doesn't stop there; it is a vicious cycle causing more stress, which, in turn, causes more inflammation, worsening the symptoms. However, this cycle can be broken!

There is a range of mindfulness exercises that can assist in lowering stress during times of abnormally high distress. Mindfulness, meditation, and breathing exercises all reduce stress in many ways. Some of the best mindfulness techniques include mindfulness-based stress reduction (MBSR), mindfulness-based cognitive therapy (MBCT), concentration meditation, mantras, guided meditations, and loving-kindness meditation.

Mindfulness allows the brain to react better to stressful situations, preventing overreactions to minor inconveniences despite being under pressure. The body benefits, as a few minutes of stepping back to practice mindfulness allows the intense fight-or-flight reaction to calm. This causes less cortisol secretion, lowering the heart rate, bringing the blood pressure back to normal range, and lowering the feeling of stress. Managing chronic stress will allow inflammation to subside, helping to diminish pain and the symptoms of autoimmune disorders such as MS and rheumatoid arthritis. Other benefits from mindfulness include increased defense against inflammatory damage, lowered pro-inflammatory processes, help with healthy aging, and teaching a person how to handle future stressful situations and cope better while under stress.

Don't forget to take a breather now and again. A few deep breaths and other breathing exercises allow you to take in more oxygen while lowering your blood pressure, releasing tension from your abdomen, slowing the heart to its normal rate, and countering the feelings associated with the fight-or-flight response.

While the immune system can malfunction and attack various parts of your body, there are many ways to help you combat it. A change in lifestyle, good food, and some supplementation will help lower the chance of intestinal permeability, leading to unwanted molecules entering your bloodstream and causing inflammation throughout your body.

Although autoimmune diseases are still being explored by science, there is no concrete evidence of a singular cause. However, one of the prevailing theories is that our Western diet is causing these and other chronic diseases to run rampant, and they aren't showing signs of slowing down. Let's recap what we have learned.

CONCLUSION

The rising number of autoimmune and chronic diseases is alarming. However, instead of trying to determine why they are occurring, the symptoms are being treated or suppressed. Not knowing what is causing the development of these diseases makes it difficult to treat what is truly wrong.

It is believed by many that the cause of autoimmune and chronic diseases is rampant inflammation caused by many different factors —ranging from stress, inactivity, smoking, and alcohol consumption to an overall poor diet. If the inflammation were controlled, the result of chronic and autoimmune diseases would indeed be controlled.

While it's strictly unknown what causes these diseases, as many factors play a role (e.g., genetics, environmental factors, and so on), science is starting to concentrate more and more on the gut microbiome and what is being fed to them.

Poor diets—high in saturated fats and additives—not only cause inflammation and dysbiosis in the gut microbiome but can lead to increased intestinal permeability, also known as leaky gut. With intestinal contents leaking into the bloodstream, the body becomes defensive, and the immune system responds. While inflammation is a sign that the body is healing, chronic inflammation—much like chronic stress—leads to problems that increase the risk of developing many diseases.

However, changing your lifestyle by being more active, stopping poor habits (e.g., excessive drinking and smoking), adopting a healthier diet, and being more mindful will improve chronic stress and inflammation and feed the gut microbiome what it needs to increase the beneficial microbiomes and diversity.

As they say, the proof is in the pudding—or, in this case, skipping pudding in favor of healthier, fiber-filled treats. Thanks to changing my diet, becoming more mindful, and not running to the doctor for every little ache and pain, I have managed to lose 72 pounds (caused by extended use of steroids), am enjoying a healthier diet with some supplements to boost my health (I'm not young anymore, after all), and I am free of diabetes, pain medications, and high blood pressure and cholesterol. I even keep up with my mindfulness daily to ensure I manage whatever stress life can throw at me.

Remember that while doctors are necessary, they shouldn't have to tell you to live healthier. That's your job. Take back your health by breaking the endless cycles of doctor's visits that only deal with the symptoms and not the problems. Start your healing journey today by taking small steps to improve your life through mindfulness, nutrition, and good food. Your life is worth extending *without* pain and sickness.

REFERENCES/BIBLIOGRAPHY

5 ways to get mindfulness into your everyday life. (n.d.). Headspace. https://www.headspace.com/articles/5-ways-to-get-mindfulness-into-your-everyday-life

8 digestive health supplements. (n.d.). WebMD. https://www.webmd.com/vitamins-and-supplements/ss/slideshow-digestive-health

Ajmera, R. (2018, October 15). *Seven health benefits and uses of anise seed*. Healthline. https://www.healthline.com/nutrition/anise

American Psychological Association. (2019, October 30). *Mindfulness meditation: A research-proven way to reduce stress*. https://www.apa.org/topics/mindfulness/meditation

Ankrom, S. (2023, January 27). *9 breathing exercises to relieve anxiety*. Verywell Mind. https://www.verywellmind.com/abdominal-breathing-2584115

Armata, N. N. (n.d.). *Dysbiosis: What is it, causes, and more*. Osmosis. https://www.osmosis.org/answers/dysbiosis

Arthritis Foundation. (n.d.). *8 food ingredients that can cause inflammation*. https://www.arthritis.org/health-wellness/healthy-living/nutrition/foods-to-limit/8-food-ingredients-that-can-cause-inflammation

Avramidou, M., Angst, F., Angst, J., Aeschlimann, A., Rössler, W., & Schnyder, U. (2018). Epidemiology of gastrointestinal symptoms in young and middle-aged Swiss adults: Prevalences and comorbidities in a longitudinal population cohort over 28 years. *BMC Gastroenterology*, *18*(21). https://doi.org/10.1186/s12876-018-0749-3

Bahls, C. (2017, June 21). *11 foods to avoid when you're having digestive problems*. Everyday Health. https://www.everydayhealth.com/digestive-health/diet/foods-to-avoid-during-digestive-problems

Bailey, C. (2019, October 10). *6 steps to heal your unhealthy gut*. Happiful. https://happiful.com/6-steps-to-heal-your-unhealthy-gut

Bax, C. E., Chakka, S., Concha, J. S. S., Zeidi, M., & Werth, V. P. (2021). The effects of immunostimulatory herbal supplements on autoimmune skin diseases. *Journal of the American Academy of Dermatology*, *84*(4), 1051–1058. https://doi.org/10.1016/j.jaad.2020.06.037

Belkaid, Y., & Hand, T. W. (2014). Role of the microbiota in immunity and inflammation. *Cell*, *157*(1), 121–141. https://doi.org/10.1016/j.cell.2014.03.011

Berry, S. (2021, June 14). *The truth about inflammation: How your diet can increase inflammation in the body*. ZOE. https://joinzoe.com/post/inflammation-ajcn

Best and worst foods for gut health (n.d.). WebMD. https://www.webmd.com/digestive-disorders/ss/slideshow-best-worst-foods-for-gut-health

Better Health Channel. (n.d.-a). *Chronic illness*. Department of Health, State of Victoria. https://www.betterhealth.vic.gov.au/health/healthyliving/chronic-illness

Better Health Channel. (n.d.-b). *Immune system explained.* Department of Health, State of Victoria. https://www.betterhealth.vic.gov.au/health/conditionsandtreatments/immune-system

Bippen, J. (2023, January 6). *Do I need supplements? 5 reasons why you might.* HUM Nutrition Blog. https://www.humnutrition.com/blog/reasons-to-take-supplements

Black, D. S., & Slavich, G. M. (2016). Mindfulness meditation and the immune system: A systematic review of randomized controlled trials. *Annals of the New York Academy of Sciences*, *1373*(1), 13–24. https://doi.org/10.1111/nyas.12998

Black, M. (2020, May 22). *How to use these 3 meditation anchors to ground your practice*. Wellness with Molly. https://wellnesswithmolly.me/blog/how-to-use-these-3-meditation-anchors-to-ground-your-practice

Bland, J. S. (2022). Therapeutic use of omega-3 fatty acids for immune disorders in search of the ideal omega-3 supplement. *Integrative Medicine (Encinitas, Calif.)*, *21*(5), 14–18. https://www.ncbi.nlm.nih.gov/pmc/articles/PMC9831136

Bolen, B. (2022, July 9). *Dysbiosis: Overview and treatment*. Verywell Health. https://www.verywellhealth.com/what-is-intestinal-dysbiosis-1945045

Bose, P. (2023, March 26). *How does diet affect inflammation?* News Medical. https://www.news-medical.net/news/20230326/How-does-diet-affect-inflammation.aspx

Brach, T. (n.d.). *How to meditate*. Tara Brach. https://www.tarabrach.com/howtomeditate

Bullock, B. G. (2020, February 20). *Mindfulness fights inflammation in stressed adults*. Mindful. https://www.mindful.org/mindfulness-fights-inflammation-in-stressed-adults

The Calmer Team. (2021, May 5). *How do breathing exercises reduce stress?* Calmer Blog. https://www.thisiscalmer.com/blog/how-do-breathing-exercises-alleviate-stress

Camilleri, M. (2019). Leaky gut: Mechanisms, measurement and clinical implications in humans. *Gut*, *68*(8), 1516–1526. https://doi.org/10.1136/gutjnl-2019-318427

Campos, M. (2023, September 12). *Leaky gut: What is it, and what does it mean for you?* Harvard Health Blog. https://www.health.harvard.edu/blog/leaky-gut-what-is-it-and-what-does-it-mean-for-you-2017092212451

Cao, C., & Brown, B. (2019). Understanding Chinese medicine and Western medicine to reach the maximum treatment benefit. *Journal of Translational Science, 6*(2). https://doi.org/10.15761/jts.1000334

Carnahan, J. (n.d.). *Leaky gut – The syndrome linked to many autoimmune diseases*. Balance Women's Health. https://balancewomenshealth.com/wp-content/uploads/2020/03/Leaky-Gut-by-Jill-Carnahan.pdf

Carter, D. (2019, March 20). *3 myths about inflammation*. MD Anderson Cancer Center. https://www.mdanderson.org/cancerwise/3-myths-about-inflammation-and-cancer.h00-159301467.html

Carver-Carter, R. (2022, May 24). *How stress impacts the microbiome and gut health*. Atlas Blog. https://atlasbiomed.com/blog/how-stress-impacts-the-gut-via-the-gut-brain-axis/

Case-Lo, C. (2023, March 27). *Food & nutrition*. Healthline. https://www.healthline.com/health/food-nutrition

Center for Mindful Psychotherapy. (2022, June 8). *Mindfulness for chronic illness: 9 ways it helps you cope*. https://mindfulcenter.org/9-ways-mindfulness-can-help-you-cope-with-chronic-illness

Centers for Disease Control and Prevention. (2022a, April 13). *What is inflammatory bowel disease (IBD)?* https://www.cdc.gov/ibd/what-is-ibd.htm

Centers for Disease Control and Prevention. (2022b, September 8). *Poor nutrition* [Fact sheet]. https://www.cdc.gov/chronicdisease/resources/publications/factsheets/nutrition.htm

Chandon, P. (2016, December 20). *The reasons we buy (and eat) too much food*. Harvard Business Review. https://hbr.org/2016/12/the-reasons-we-buy-and-eat-too-much-food

Chandrasekaran, A., Molparia, B., Akhtar, E., Wang, X., Lewis, J. D., Chang, J. T., Oliveira, G., Torkamani, A., & Konijeti, G. G. (2019). The autoimmune protocol diet modifies intestinal RNA expression in inflammatory bowel disease. *Crohn's & Colitis* 360, *1*(3). https://doi.org/10.1093/crocol/otz016

Charles Alexis, A. (2022, April 13). *Can food be medicine? Pros and cons*. Medical News Today. https://www.medicalnewstoday.com/articles/can-food-be-medicine-pros-and-cons

Cherney, K. (2020, November 15). *9 herbs to fight arthritis pain*. Healthline. https://www.healthline.com/health/osteoarthritis/herbs-arthritis-pain

Chervil – Uses, side effects, and more. (n.d.). WebMD. https://www.webmd.com/vitamins/ai/ingredientmono-250/chervil

Christovich, A., & Luo, X. M. (2022). Gut microbiota, leaky gut, and autoimmune diseases. *Frontiers in Immunology, 13*. https://doi.org/10.3389/fimmu.2022.946248

Cleveland Clinic. (n.d.-a). *Crohn's disease*. https://my.clevelandclinic.org/health/diseases/9357-crohns-disease

Cleveland Clinic. (n.d.-b). *Immune system.* https://my.clevelandclinic.org/health/articles/21196-immune-system

Cleveland Clinic. (2023a, January 30). *How to practice mindful eating.* https://health.clevelandclinic.org/mindful-eating

Cleveland Clinic. (2023b, August 3). *31 high-fiber foods you should be eating.* https://health.clevelandclinic.org/high-fiber-foods

Cleveland Clinic. (2023c, September 20). *Chronic illness.* https://my.clevelandclinic.org/health/articles/4062-chronic-illness

Cleveland Clinic. (2023d, September 20). *Digestive system.* https://my.clevelandclinic.org/health/body/7041-digestive-system

Cleveland Clinic. (2023e, September 20). *Inflammation.* https://my.clevelandclinic.org/health/symptoms/21660-inflammation

Cleveland Clinic. (2023f, September 20). *Inflammatory bowel disease (overview).* https://my.clevelandclinic.org/health/diseases/15587-inflammatory-bowel-disease-overview

Cleveland Clinic. (2023g, September 20). *Leaky gut syndrome.* https://my.clevelandclinic.org/health/diseases/22724-leaky-gut-syndrome

Cohen, S. (2021, March 19). *If you want to boost immunity, look to the gut.* UCLA Health. https://www.uclahealth.org/news/want-to-boost-immunity-look-to-the-gut

Counseling and Psychological Services. (n.d.). *Stress and the digestive system.* Brigham Young University. https://caps.byu.edu/stress-and-the-digestive-system

Coyle, D. (2017, June 19). *8 surprising things that harm your gut bacteria.* Healthline. https://www.healthline.com/nutrition/8-things-that-harm-gut-bacteria

Cross, P. I. (2023, January 18). *Deep meditation: Might it change the gut microbiome to boost health?* Medical News Today. https://www.medicalnewstoday.com/articles/deep-meditation-might-it-change-the-gut-microbiome-to-boost-health

Cuncic, A. (2021, October 26). *What is 4-7-8 breathing?* Verywell Mind. https://www.verywellmind.com/what-is-4-7-8-breathing-5204438

Daniel, C. (2022, April 10). *A look inside your digestive system.* Verywell Health. https://www.verywellhealth.com/tour-the-digestive-system-4020262

Darian, M. (2023, May 26). *9 foods to avoid on the autoimmune protocol with autoimmune diseases.* Well Theory. https://www.welltheory.com/resources/foods-to-avoid-with-autoimmune-diseases

Davis, D. M., & Hayes, J. A. (2012). What are the benefits of mindfulness? *Monitor on Psychology*, *43*(7), 64. https://www.apa.org/monitor/2012/07-08/ce-corner

de Jong, P. R., González-Navajas, J. M., & Jansen, N. J. G. (2016). The digestive tract as the origin of systemic inflammation. *Critical Care*, *20*(279). https://doi.org/10.1186/s13054-016-1458-3

de Vibe, M., Bjørndal, A., Fattah, S., Dyrdal, G. M., Halland, E., & Tanner-Smith, E.

E. (2017). Mindfulness-based stress reduction (MBSR) for improving health, quality of life and social functioning in adults: A systematic review and meta-analysis. *Campbell Systematic Reviews*, *13*(1), 1–264. https://doi.org/10.4073/csr.2017.11

DeGruttola, A. K., Low, D., Mizoguchi, A., & Mizoguchi, E. (2016). Current understanding of dysbiosis in disease in human and animal models. *Inflammatory Bowel Diseases*, *22*(5), 1137–1150. https://doi.org/10.1097/mib.0000000000000750

[Deleted]. (2022, July 4). *Fibromyalgia and mindfulness – your experiences?* [Online forum post]. Reddit. https://www.reddit.com/r/Fibromyalgia/comments/vr84xq/comment/ietv37e

Denhard, M. (2022, February 10). *Digestive enzymes and digestive enzyme supplements*. Johns Hopkins Medicine. https://www.hopkinsmedicine.org/health/wellness-and-prevention/digestive-enzymes-and-digestive-enzyme-supplements

Deshmukh, R. K. (2016, November 12). *Unhealthy food you should try to avoid*. Practo. https://www.practo.com/healthfeed/unhealthy-food-you-should-try-to-avoid-25522/post

Dey, E. (2015, May 13). *Buddha belly: Meditation may ease gut ailments*. Live Science. https://www.livescience.com/50816-meditation-ease-gut-disorders.html

Didelot, X., Walker, A. S., Peto, T. E., Crook, D. W., & Wilson, D. J. (2016). Within-host evolution of bacterial pathogens. *Nature Reviews Microbiology*, *14*(3), 150–162. https://doi.org/10.1038/nrmicro.2015.13

Dimitratos, S. (2018, March 16). *Inflammation: What is it, and how can my diet and behavior affect it?* American Society for Nutrition. https://nutrition.org/inflammation-what-is-it-and-how-can-my-diet-and-behavior-affect-it

Dougherty, A. (2019, June 17). *Meditation & its impact on gut health*. Gutbliss. https://gutbliss.com/meditation-its-impact-on-gut-health

Downey, M. (2023, August). *Probiotics provide vital protection against chronic disease*. Life Extension. https://www.lifeextension.com/magazine/2014/5/probiotics-provide-vital-protection-against-chronic-disease

Drees, B. M., & Barthel, B. (2022). We are what we eat. *Missouri Medicine*, *119*(5), 479–480. https://www.ncbi.nlm.nih.gov/pmc/articles/PMC9616445

Duggan, K. F. (2018, November 16). *Ten healthy eating rules from a nutritionist*. One Medical. https://www.onemedical.com/blog/eat-well/healthy-eating-checklist

Dursteler, E. R. (2022, April 28). *Food and identity in Europe past and present*. Kennedy Center. https://kennedy.byu.edu/alumni/bridges/features/you-are-what-you-eat

Early, K. B. & Stanley, K. (2018). Position of the academy of nutrition and dietetics: The role of medical nutrition therapy and registered dietitian nutritionists in the prevention and treatment of prediabetes and type 2 diabetes. *Journal of the Academy of Nutrition and Dietetics, 118*(2), 343–353. https://doi.org/10.1016/j.jand.2017.11.021

The Editors of Encyclopedia Britannica. (n.d.). *Is inflammation good or bad?* Encyclopedia Britannica. https://www.britannica.com/question/Is-inflammation-good-or-bad

Erickson, K. (2021, January 7). *Gut health and inflammation: What's the connection?* Fullscript. https://fullscript.com/blog/gut-health-and-inflammation

Eske, J. (2023, January 6). *What to know about leaky gut syndrome*. Medical News Today. https://www.medicalnewstoday.com/articles/326117

familydoctor.org editorial staff. (2022, April 18). *Changing your diet: Choosing nutrient-rich foods*. familydoctor.org. https://familydoctor.org/changing-your-diet-choosing-nutrient-rich-foods

Felman, A. (2023, April 14). *Everything you need to know about inflammation*. Medical News Today. https://www.medicalnewstoday.com/articles/248423

Fletcher, J. (2023, September 6). *Anti-inflammatory diet: What to know*. Medical News Today. https://www.medicalnewstoday.com/articles/320233

Furman, D., Campisi, J., Verdin, E., Carrera-Bastos, P., Targ, S., Franceschi, C., Ferrucci, L., Gilroy, D. W., Fasano, A., Miller, G. W., Miller, A. H., Mantovani, A., Weyand, C. M., Barzilai, N., Goronzy, J. J., Rando, T. A., Effros, R. B., Lucia, A., Kleinstreuer, N., & Slavich, G. M. (2019). Chronic inflammation in the etiology of disease across the life span. *Nature Medicine*, *25*(12), 1822–1832. https://doi.org/10.1038/s41591-019-0675-0

Gallego, A. (n.d.). *How diet affects your gut microbiome*. GoldBio. https://goldbio.com/articles/article/Diet-Affects-Gut-Microbiome

Gawley, J. (2022, August 24). *Top 10 supplements for digestive health*. Life Extension. https://www.lifeextension.com/wellness/supplements/10-best-gut-health-supplements

Good Food Is Good Medicine. (2019, April 5). *Top 15 healthy foods you should be eating*. UC Davis Health. https://health.ucdavis.edu/blog/good-food/top-15-healthy-foods-you-should-be-eating/2019/04

Gora, A. (2022, September 13). *Probiotics vs digestive enzymes: What's the difference?* Live Science. https://www.livescience.com/probiotics-vs-digestive-enzymes

Gout. (2022, November 29). Hospital for Special Surgery. https://www.hss.edu/condition-list_gout.asp

Gregoire, C. (2016, February 8). *Here's how meditation reduces inflammation and prevents disease*. HuffPost. https://www.huffpost.com/entry/meditation-brain-changes-study_n_56b4b7aee4b04f9b57d93bef

Gregory, A. (2023, January 17). *Meditation could have positive impact on gut and overall health*. The Guardian. https://www.theguardian.com/lifeandstyle/2023/jan/17/meditation-could-have-positive-impact-on-gut-overall-health-microbiome

Groves, M. (2023, March 13). *The 11 best ways to improve your digestion naturally*. Healthline. https://www.healthline.com/nutrition/ways-to-improve-digestion

Gunnars, K. (2019, February 27). *Does all disease begin in your gut? The surprising truth*. Healthline. https://www.healthline.com/nutrition/does-all-disease-begin-in-the-gut

Gut health foods – 15 foods for good gut health. (n.d.). Benenden Health. https://www.benenden.co.uk/be-healthy/nutrition/gut-food-15-foods-for-good-gut-health/

Haller, E. (2022, June 15). *Dietary interventions for gastrointestinal disorders*. International Foundation for Gastrointestinal Disorders. https://iffgd.org/norton-education-series/nes-education-30-anniversary/11563-2-5-2-4-2

Harkins, P., Burke, E., Swales, C., & Silman, A. (2021). 'All disease begins in the gut'—The role of the intestinal microbiome in ankylosing spondylitis. *Rheumatology Advances in Practice*, *5*(3). https://doi.org/10.1093/rap/rkab063

Harvard Health Publishing. (2016a, January 16). *8 steps to mindful eating*. Staying Healthy. https://www.health.harvard.edu/staying-healthy/8-steps-to-mindful-eating

Harvard Health Publishing. (2016b, October 28). *Which foods don't belong in a healthy diet?* Staying Healthy. https://www.health.harvard.edu/staying-healthy/which-foods-dont-belong-in-a-healthy-diet

Harvard Health Publishing. (2021a, February 12). *Do you need a daily supplement?* Staying Healthy. https://www.health.harvard.edu/staying-healthy/do-you-need-a-daily-supplement

Harvard Health Publishing. (2021b, April 12). *What is Inflammation?* Ask the Doctor. https://www.health.harvard.edu/newsletter_article/ask-the-doctor-what-is-inflammation

Harvard Health Publishing. (2021c, November 16). *Foods that fight inflammation*. Staying Healthy. https://www.health.harvard.edu/staying-healthy/foods-that-fight-inflammation

Harvard Health Publishing. (2022, October 20). *Inflammation myths and misconceptions*. Healthbeat. https://www.health.harvard.edu/healthbeat/inflammation-myths-and-misconceptions

Harvard School of Public Health. (2019, November 4). *Whole grains*. The Nutrition Source. https://www.hsph.harvard.edu/nutritionsource/what-should-you-eat/whole-grains

Harvard School of Public Health. (2022a, July 25). *The microbiome*. The Nutrition Source. https://www.hsph.harvard.edu/nutritionsource/microbiome

Harvard School of Public Health. (2022b, December 5). *Nutrition and immunity*. The

Nutrition Source. https://www.hsph.harvard.edu/nutritionsource/nutrition-and-immunity

Harvard School of Public Health. (2023a, February 2). *Diet review: Anti-Inflammatory diet*. The Nutrition Source. https://www.hsph.harvard.edu/nutritionsource/healthy-weight/diet-reviews/anti-inflammatory-diet

Harvard School of Public Health. (2023b, March 7). *Chloride*. The Nutrition Source. https://www.hsph.harvard.edu/nutritionsource/chloride

Harvard School of Public Health. (2023c, March 7). *Niacin – Vitamin B3*. The Nutrition Source. https://www.hsph.harvard.edu/nutritionsource/niacin-vitamin-b3

Harvard School of Public Health. (2023d, July 14). *Mindful eating*. The Nutrition Source. https://www.hsph.harvard.edu/nutritionsource/mindful-eating

Health for Life. (n.d.). *Focus on wellness*. https://www.aha.org/system/files/content/00-10/071204_H4L_FocusonWellness.pdf

Healthy eating and the digestive system. (2021, May 24). Guts UK. https://gutscharity.org.uk/advice-and-information/health-and-lifestyle/diet

Henry Ford Health Staff. (2018, May 11). *Inflammation and your diet: What's the connection?* Henry Ford Health. https://www.henryford.com/blog/2018/05/inflammation-and-your-diet-whats-the-connection

Henry Ford Health Staff. (2021, July 26). *How stress affects digestion—and what you can do about it*. Henry Ford Health. https://www.henryford.com/blog/2021/07/how-stress-affects-digestion

Hill, A. (2019, December 6). *Everything you need to know about caraway*. Healthline. https://www.healthline.com/nutrition/caraway

Hill, A. (2023, July 13). *Star anise: Benefits, uses and potential risks*. Healthline. https://www.healthline.com/nutrition/star-anise

Hill, L. (2022, March 28). *Signs of an unhealthy gut*. UNC Health Pardee. https://healthywithpardee.com/signs-of-an-unhealthy-gut

Hills, R. D., Pontefract, B. A., Mishcon, H. R., Black, C. A., Sutton, S. C., & Theberge, C. R. (2019). Gut microbiome: Profound implications for diet and disease. *Nutrients*, *11*(7), 1613. https://doi.org/10.3390/nu11071613

Hippocrates. (n.d.) *Hippocrates quotes*. Quotefancy. https://quotefancy.com/quote/829226/Hippocrates-The-greatest-medicine-of-all-is-teaching-people-how-not-to-need-it

Hoffman, M. (2010, November 29). *What is an autoimmune disease?* WebMD. https://www.webmd.com/a-to-z-guides/autoimmune-diseases

Hoshaw, C. (2022a, March 29). *What is mindfulness? A simple practice for greater wellbeing*. Healthline. https://www.healthline.com/health/mind-body/what-is-mindfulness

Hoshaw, C. (2022b, June 22). *32 mindfulness activities to find calm at any age*. Healthline. https://www.healthline.com/health/mind-body/mindfulness-activities

Houghton, T. [Sam] (2021, July 23). *Autoimmunity and diet: Is there a connection?* Center for Nutrition Studies. https://nutritionstudies.org/autoimmunity-and-diet-is-there-a-connection

How cancer is treated. (n.d.). Cancer.Net. https://www.cancer.net/navigating-cancer-care/how-cancer-treated/conventional-cancer-treatments/side-effects-cancer-treatment

How your gut health affects your whole body. (n.d.). WebMD. https://www.webmd.com/digestive-disorders/ss/slideshow-how-gut-health-affects-whole-body

Hrncir, T. (2022). Gut microbiota dysbiosis: Triggers, consequences, diagnostic and therapeutic options. *Microorganisms*, *10*(3), 578. https://doi.org/10.3390/microorganisms10030578

The human body's ability to self-heal. (n.d.). Tummy Calm. https://www.tummycalm.com/self-healing.html

Iftikhar, N. (2022, July 25). *What is allopathic medicine?* Healthline. https://www.healthline.com/health/allopathic-medicine

Inflammatory disorders. (2022, October 6). Hospital for Special Surgery. https://www.hss.edu/condition-list_inflammatory-disorders.asp

Institute of Medicine (US) Committee on Diet and Health. Woteki, C. E., & Thomas, P. R. (Eds). (1992). *Eat for life: The food and nutrition board's guide to reducing your risk of chronic disease*. National Academy Press. https://www.ncbi.nlm.nih.gov/books/NBK235010

Jadhav, P., Jiang, Y., Jarr, K., Layton, C., Ashouri, J. F., & Sinha, S. R. (2020). Efficacy of dietary supplements in inflammatory bowel disease and related autoimmune diseases. *Nutrients*, *12*(7), 2156. https://doi.org/10.3390/nu12072156

Janeway, C. A., Travers, P., Walport, M., & Shlomchik, M. J. (2001). *Immunobiology* (5th ed.). Garland Science. https://livresbioapp.files.wordpress.com/2015/07/janeway-c-travers-p-walport-m-shlomchik-m-immunobiology-2001.pdf

Jennings, K.-A., & Mathis, A. (2023, July 18). *14 of the world's healthiest spices & herbs you should be eating*. EatingWell. https://www.eatingwell.com/article/32764/eight-of-the-worlds-healthiest-spices-herbs-you-should-be-eating

Jiang, T. A. (2019, November 23). Health benefits of culinary herbs and spices. *Journal of AOAC International*, *102*(2), 395–411. https://doi.org/10.5740/jaoacint.18-0418

Johns Hopkins Medicine. (n.d.-a). *Definition of autoimmunity & autoimmune disease*. https://pathology.jhu.edu/autoimmune/definitions

Johns Hopkins Medicine. (n.d.-b). *Inclusion body myositis*. https://www.hopkinsmedicine.org/health/conditions-and-diseases/inclusion-body-myositis

Johns Hopkins Medicine. (2019a). *Amyotrophic lateral sclerosis (ALS)*. https://www.hopkinsmedicine.org/health/conditions-and-diseases/amyotrophic-lateral-sclerosis-als

Johns Hopkins Medicine. (2019b). *5 foods to improve your digestion*. https://www.hopkinsmedicine.org/health/wellness-and-prevention/5-foods-to-improve-your-digestion

Johns Hopkins Medicine. (2019c). *The immune system*. https://www.hopkinsmedicine.org/health/conditions-and-diseases/the-immune-system

Johns Hopkins Medicine. (2021). *Intermittent fasting: What is it, and how does it work?* https://www.hopkinsmedicine.org/health/wellness-and-prevention/intermittent-fasting-what-is-it-and-how-does-it-work

Jones, L. (2013, February 15). *HEALING—The human body is a self-healing organism*. Norfolk Wellness. https://norfolkwellness.com/blog/healing.htm

Joo, J. Y. (2023). Fragmented care and chronic illness patient outcomes: A systematic review. *Nursing Open*, *10*(6) 3460–3473. https://doi.org/10.1002/nop2.1607

Katella, K. (2020, August 31). *Do you really need all of those medications?* Yale Medicine. https://www.yalemedicine.org/news/polyphamacy

Kest, B. (2021, August 10). *Disadvantages of Western medicine*. Power Yoga. https://poweryoga.com/the-absurdity-of-western-medicine/

Konijeti, G. G., Kim, N., Lewis, J. D., Groven, S., Chandrasekaran, A., Grandhe, S., Diamant, C., Singh, E., Oliveira, G., Wang, X., Molparia, B., & Torkamani, A. (2017, September 29). Efficacy of the autoimmune protocol diet for inflammatory bowel disease. *Inflammatory Bowel Diseases*, *23*(11), 2054–2060. https://doi.org/10.1097/mib.0000000000001221

Kubala, J. (2019, June 12). *8 science-backed benefits of nutmeg*. Healthline. https://www.healthline.com/nutrition/nutmeg-benefits

Kurup, S., & Pozun, A. (2022, December 19). *Biochemistry, autoimmunity*. PubMed. https://www.ncbi.nlm.nih.gov/books/NBK576418

Lang, A. (2021, September 24). *Allspice — A unique spice with surprising health benefits*. Healthline. https://www.healthline.com/nutrition/allspice

Laurence, E. (2020, March 16). *The 10-minute wellness habit that fights inflammation*. Well+Good. https://www.wellandgood.com/meditation-inflammation

Le Guillou, I. (2021, February 2). *Why gut bacteria are becoming key suspects in autoimmune diseases*. Horizon. https://ec.europa.eu/research-and-innovation/en/horizon-magazine/why-gut-bacteria-are-becoming-key-suspects-autoimmune-diseases

Lee, Y., Cho, J., Sohn, J., & Kim, C. (2023). Health effects of microplastic exposures: Current issues and perspectives in South Korea. *Yonsei Medical Journal, 64*(5), 301–308. https://doi.org/10.3349/ymj.2023.0048

Lehman, S. (2023, January 19). *Benefits and risks of dietary supplements.* Verywell Fit. https://www.verywellfit.com/benefits-and-risks-of-taking-dietary-supplements-2506547

Lehman, S., & Pine, M. D. (2022, December 30). *Tips for how to take your vitamins.* Nature Made. https://www.naturemade.com/blogs/health-articles/tips-for-how-to-take-your-vitamins

Lenkin, E. (2018, January 12). *4 ways to anchor your focus in meditation.* Fit Bottomed Girls. https://fitbottomedgirls.com/2018/01/4-ways-to-anchor-your-focus-in-meditation

Lennon, A. (2022, February 2). *Vitamin D and fish oil supplements reduce risk of autoimmune conditions.* Medical News Today. https://www.medicalnewstoday.com/articles/vitamin-d-and-fish-oil-supplements-reduce-risk-of-autoimmune-conditions

Livovsky, D. M., Pribic, T., & Azpiroz, F. (2020). Food, eating, and the gastrointestinal tract. *Nutrients, 12*(4), 986. https://doi.org/10.3390/nu12040986

Lockett, E. (2019, February 26). *Leaky gut supplements: What you need to know to feel better.* Healthline. https://www.healthline.com/health/digestive-health/leaky-gut-supplements

LoveBug Probiotics. (2021, December 18). *13 foods that are terrible for your gut health.* https://lovebugprobiotics.com/blogs/news/13-foods-that-are-terrible-for-your-gut-health

Lupus. (2023, June 5). Hospital for Special Surgery. https://www.hss.edu/condition-list_lupus.asp

Mace – Uses, side effects, and more. (n.d.). WebMD. https://www.webmd.com/vitamins/ai/ingredientmono-1530/mace

Maguire, H. (2015, November 19). *Choosing and using your anchor in meditation.* So Mindful. http://so-mindful.co.uk/benefits-of-mindfulness/choosing-and-using-your-anchor-in-meditation/

Maiese, E. M., Evans, K. A., Chu, B.-C., & Irwin, D. E. (2018). Temporal trends in survival and healthcare costs in patients with multiple myeloma in the United States. *American Health & Drug Benefits, 11*(1), 39–46. https://www.ncbi.nlm.nih.gov/pmc/articles/PMC5902764

Manzel, A., Muller, D. N., Hafler, D. A., Erdman, S. E., Linker, R. A., & Kleinewietfeld, M. (2014). Role of "Western diet" in inflammatory autoimmune diseases. *Current Allergy and Asthma Reports, 14*(404). https://doi.org/10.1007/s11882-013-0404-6

Marchant, J. (2017, June 16). *Mindfulness and meditation dampen down inflamma-*

tion genes. New Scientist. https://www.newscientist.com/article/2137595-mindfulness-and-meditation-dampen-down-inflammation-genes

Martin, L. (2021, October 14). *What to know about allopathic medicine*. Medical News Today. https://www.medicalnewstoday.com/articles/allopathic-medicine

Mayo Clinic Staff. (2021, October 26). *Fibromyalgia*. Mayo Clinic. https://www.mayoclinic.org/diseases-conditions/fibromyalgia/symptoms-causes/syc-20354780

Mayo Clinic Staff. (2022a, January 15). *Hashimoto's disease*. Mayo Clinic. https://www.mayoclinic.org/diseases-conditions/hashimotos-disease/symptoms-causes/syc-20351855

Mayo Clinic Staff. (2022b, June 14). *Graves' disease*. Mayo Clinic. https://www.mayoclinic.org/diseases-conditions/graves-disease/symptoms-causes/syc-20356240

Mayo Clinic Staff. (2022c, September 16). *Ulcerative colitis*. Mayo Clinic. https://www.mayoclinic.org/diseases-conditions/ulcerative-colitis/symptoms-causes/syc-20353326

Mayo Clinic Staff. (2022d, October 8). *Psoriasis*. Mayo Clinic. https://www.mayoclinic.org/diseases-conditions/psoriasis/symptoms-causes/syc-20355840

Mayo Clinic Staff. (2022e, October 11). *Mindfulness exercises*. Mayo Clinic. https://www.mayoclinic.org/healthy-lifestyle/consumer-health/in-depth/mindfulness-exercises/art-20046356

Mayo Clinic Staff. (2022f, December 24). *Multiple sclerosis*. Mayo Clinic. https://www.mayoclinic.org/diseases-conditions/multiple-sclerosis/symptoms-causes/syc-20350269

Mayo Clinic Staff. (2023a, January 4). *Gastroesophageal reflux disease (GERD)*. Mayo Clinic. https://www.mayoclinic.org/diseases-conditions/gerd/symptoms-causes/syc-20361940

Mayo Clinic Staff. (2023b, January 25). *Rheumatoid arthritis*. Mayo Clinic. https://www.mayoclinic.org/diseases-conditions/rheumatoid-arthritis/symptoms-causes/syc-20353648

Mayo Clinic Staff. (2023c, May 12). *Irritable bowel syndrome*. Mayo Clinic. https://www.mayoclinic.org/diseases-conditions/irritable-bowel-syndrome/symptoms-causes/syc-20360016

Mayo Clinic Staff. (2023d, September 12). *Celiac disease*. Mayo Clinic. https://www.mayoclinic.org/diseases-conditions/celiac-disease/symptoms-causes/syc-20352220

Mazzucca, C. B., Raineri, D., Cappellano, G., & Chiocchetti, A. (2021). How to tackle the relationship between autoimmune diseases and diet: Well begun is half-done. *Nutrients*, *13*(11), 3956. https://doi.org/10.3390/nu13113956

McCallum, K. (2022, June 29). *5 types of foods that cause inflammation*. Houston

Methodist. https://www.houstonmethodist.org/blog/articles/2022/jun/5-types-of-foods-that-cause-inflammation

McCoy, K. (2023, September 7). *Leaky gut syndrome: 7 signs you may have it.* Dr. Axe. https://draxe.com/health/7-signs-symptoms-you-have-leaky-gut

McGrane, K. (2020, February 4). *All you need to know about dill.* Healthline. https://www.healthline.com/nutrition/dill

McMillen, M. (2016, April 14). *Nick Cannon: A warrior in the fight against lupus.* WebMD. https://www.webmd.com/lupus/features/nick-cannon-lupus

MedicineNet. (2014, May 2). *MedTerms medical dictionary A-Z list – A.* https://www.medicinenet.com/script/main/alphaidx.asp?p=a_dict

Miller, K. (2023, January 22). *Study finds meditation may improve your gut health over time.* Prevention. https://www.prevention.com/health/a42555858/deep-meditation-gut-health

Mindful eating. (2013). Headspace. https://www.headspace.com/mindfulness/mindful-eating

Mindful Staff. (2022, August 31). *The ultimate guide to the research on the effects of mindfulness and meditation for our health, psyche, and overall quality of life.* Mindful. https://www.mindful.org/the-science-of-mindfulness

Modi, J. (2021, September 20). *Foods to avoid if you have an autoimmune condition.* BuzzRx. https://www.buzzrx.com/blog/foods-to-avoid-if-you-have-an-autoimmune-condition

Mousa, W. K., Chehadeh, F., & Husband, S. (2022, October 20). Microbial dysbiosis in the gut drives systemic autoimmune diseases. *Frontiers in Immunology, 13.* https://doi.org/10.3389/fimmu.2022.906258

Mymee. (2022, April 11). *About autoimmune conditions and stress.* https://www.mymee.com/blog/about-autoimmune-conditions-and-stress

Nall, R. (2023, March 17). *What are the best foods to aid digestion?* Medical News Today. https://www.medicalnewstoday.com/articles/326596

Nania, R. (2022, June 16). *Dietary supplements and side effects.* AARP. https://www.aarp.org/health/drugs-supplements/info-2022/supplement-side-effects.html

National Cancer Institute. (2023, June 12). *Complementary and alternative medicine.* US Department of Health and Human Services, National Institutes of Health. https://www.cancer.gov/about-cancer/treatment/cam

National Center for Complementary and Integrative Health. (2017, September). *Naturopathy.* US Department of Health and Human Services, National Institutes of Health. https://www.nccih.nih.gov/health/naturopathy

National Center for Complementary and Integrative Health. (2019a, January). *Ayurvedic medicine: In depth.* US Department of Health and Human Services, National Institutes of Health. https://www.nccih.nih.gov/health/ayurvedic-medicine-in-depth

National Center for Complementary and Integrative Health. (2019b, April). *Traditional Chinese medicine: What you need to know.* US Department of Health and Human Services, National Institutes of Health. https://www.nccih.nih.gov/health/traditional-chinese-medicine-what-you-need-to-know

National Center for Complementary and Integrative Health. (2020a, August). *Fenugreek.* US Department of Health and Human Services, National Institutes of Health. https://www.nccih.nih.gov/health/fenugreek

National Center for Complementary and Integrative Health. (2020b, October). *Sage.* US Department of Health and Human Services, National Institutes of Health. https://www.nccih.nih.gov/health/sage

National Center for Complementary and Integrative Health. (2021, April). *Homeopathy: What you need to know.* US Department of Health and Human Services, National Institutes of Health. https://www.nccih.nih.gov/health/homeopathy

National Center for Complementary and Integrative Health. (2022, June). *Meditation and mindfulness: What you need to know.* US Department of Health and Human Services, National Institutes of Health. https://www.nccih.nih.gov/health/meditation-and-mindfulness-what-you-need-to-know

National Center for Complementary and Integrative Health. (2023a, September 26). *8 things to know about meditation and mindfulness.* US Department of Health and Human Services, National Institutes of Health. https://www.nccih.nih.gov/health/tips/8-things-to-know-about-meditation-and-mindfulness

National Center for Complementary and Integrative Health. (2023b, September 26). *Mind and body approaches for chronic pain.* US Department of Health and Human Services, National Institutes of Health. https://www.nccih.nih.gov/health/providers/digest/mind-and-body-approaches-for-chronic-pain

National Institute of Diabetes And Digestive And Kidney Diseases. (n.d.). *Digestive diseases.* US Department of Health and Human Services, National Institutes of Health. https://www.niddk.nih.gov/health-information/digestive-diseases

National Institute of Diabetes and Digestive and Kidney Diseases. (2017, December). *Your digestive system & how it works.* US Department of Health and Human Services, National Institutes of Health. https://www.niddk.nih.gov/health-information/digestive-diseases/digestive-system-how-it-works

National Institute of Environmental Health Sciences. (2022, May 31). *Autoimmune diseases.* US Department of Health and Human Services, National Institutes of Health. https://www.niehs.nih.gov/health/topics/conditions/autoimmune

National Institutes of Health. (2022, September 12) Physiology, Digestion. https://www.ncbi.nlm.nih.gov/books/NBK544242/

National Institutes of Health. (n.d.). *ODS videos.* https://ods.od.nih.gov/About/ODS_Videos.aspx

National Institutes of Health. (2020a, March 11). *Background information: Dietary supplements* [Fact sheet]. https://ods.od.nih.gov/factsheets/DietarySupplements-Consumer

National Institutes of Health. (2020b, December 11). *Botanical dietary supplements background information* [Fact sheet]. https://ods.od.nih.gov/factsheets/BotanicalBackground-Consumer

National Institutes of Health. (2021a, March 26). *Pantothenic acid* [Fact sheet]. https://ods.od.nih.gov/factsheets/PantothenicAcid-HealthProfessional

National Institutes of Health. (2021b, March 26). *Selenium* [Fact sheet]. https://ods.od.nih.gov/factsheets/selenium-healthprofessional

National Institutes of Health. (2021c, March 26). *Vitamin C* [Fact sheet]. https://ods.od.nih.gov/factsheets/VitaminC-HealthProfessional

National Institutes of Health. (2021d, March 26). *Vitamin E* [Fact sheet]. https://ods.od.nih.gov/factsheets/VitaminE-HealthProfessional

National Institutes of Health. (2021e, March 29). *Manganese* [Fact sheet]. https://ods.od.nih.gov/factsheets/Manganese-HealthProfessional

National Institutes of Health. (2021f, March 29). *Vitamin K* [Fact sheet]. https://ods.od.nih.gov/factsheets/vitaminK-HealthProfessional

National Institutes of Health. (2022a, January 10). *Biotin* [Fact sheet]. https://ods.od.nih.gov/factsheets/Biotin-HealthProfessional

National Institutes of Health. (2022b, April 26). *Fluoride* [Fact sheet]. https://ods.od.nih.gov/factsheets/Fluoride-HealthProfessional

National Institutes of Health. (2022c, April 28). *Iodine* [Fact sheet]. https://ods.od.nih.gov/factsheets/Iodine-HealthProfessional

National Institutes of Health. (2022d, May 11). *Riboflavin* [Fact sheet]. https://ods.od.nih.gov/factsheets/Riboflavin-HealthProfessional

National Institutes of Health. (2022e, June 2). *Chromium* [Fact sheet]. https://ods.od.nih.gov/factsheets/Chromium-HealthProfessional

National Institutes of Health. (2022f, June 2). *Magnesium* [Fact sheet]. https://ods.od.nih.gov/factsheets/Magnesium-HealthProfessional

National Institutes of Health. (2022g, June 2). *Potassium* [Fact sheet]. https://ods.od.nih.gov/factsheets/Potassium-HealthProfessional

National Institutes of Health. (2022h, June 15). *Vitamin A and carotenoids* [Fact sheet]. https://ods.od.nih.gov/factsheets/VitaminA-HealthProfessional

National Institutes of Health. (2022i, August 12). *Vitamin D* [Fact sheet]. https://ods.od.nih.gov/factsheets/VitaminD-HealthProfessional

National Institutes of Health. (2022j, September 28). *Zinc* [Fact sheet]. https://ods.od.nih.gov/factsheets/Zinc-HealthProfessional

National Institutes of Health. (2022k, October 6). *Calcium* [Fact sheet]. https://ods.od.nih.gov/factsheets/Calcium-HealthProfessional

National Institutes of Health. (2022l, October 18). *Copper* [Fact sheet]. https://ods.od.nih.gov/factsheets/Copper-HealthProfessional

National Institutes of Health. (2022m, November 18). *Niacin* [Fact sheet]. https://ods.od.nih.gov/factsheets/Niacin-HealthProfessional

National Institutes of Health. (2022n, November 30). *Folate* [Fact sheet]. https://ods.od.nih.gov/factsheets/Folate-HealthProfessional

National Institutes of Health. (2022o, December 22). *Vitamin B12* [Fact sheet]. https://ods.od.nih.gov/factsheets/VitaminB12-HealthProfessional

National Institutes of Health. (2023a, January 4). *Dietary supplements: What you need to know* [Fact sheet]. https://ods.od.nih.gov/factsheets/WYNTK-Consumer

National Institutes of Health. (2023b, February 9). *Thiamin* [Fact sheet]. https://ods.od.nih.gov/factsheets/Thiamin-HealthProfessional

National Institutes of Health. (2023c, March 21). *Frequently asked questions (FAQ)*. https://ods.od.nih.gov/HealthInformation/ODS_Frequently_Asked_Questions.aspx

National Institutes of Health. (2023d, June 15). *Iron* [Fact sheet]. https://ods.od.nih.gov/factsheets/Iron-HealthProfessional

National Institutes of Health. (2023e, June 2016). *Vitamin B6* [Fact sheet]. https://ods.od.nih.gov/factsheets/vitaminB6-healthprofessional

National Library of Medicine. (2020, April 23). *How does the immune system work?* US Department of Health and Human Services, National Institutes of Health. https://www.ncbi.nlm.nih.gov/books/NBK279364

Neff, K. D. (2022). Self-Compassion: Theory, method, research, and intervention. *Annual Review of Psychology*, *74*(1), 193–218. https://doi.org/10.1146/annurev-psych-032420-031047

Nelson, J. B. (2017). Mindful eating: The art of presence while you eat. *Diabetes Spectrum*, *30*(3), 171–174. https://doi.org/10.2337/ds17-0015

News in Health. (2019, October 4). *Keeping your gut in check.* US Department of Health and Human Services, National Institutes of Health. https://newsinhealth.nih.gov/2017/05/keeping-your-gut-check

News Medical. (2020, May 27). *Study shows global prevalence of functional gastrointestinal disorders.* https://www.news-medical.net/news/20200527/Study-shows-global-prevalence-of-functional-gastrointestinal-disorders.aspx

Novakovic, A. (2023, March 31). *What are the most healthy foods?* Medical News Today. https://www.medicalnewstoday.com/articles/245259

O'Neill Hayes, T., & Gillian, S. (2020, November 16). *Background: Understanding the connections between chronic disease and individual-level risk factors.* American Action Forum. https://www.americanactionforum.org/research/background-understanding-the-connections-between-chronic-disease-and-individual-level-risk-factors

Operation Supplement Safety. (2021, July 12). *Ashwagandha in dietary supplement products*. https://www.opss.org/article/ashwagandha-dietary-supplement-products

Orbai, A.-M. (n.d.). *What are common symptoms of autoimmune disease?* Johns Hopkins Medicine. https://www.hopkinsmedicine.org/health/wellness-and-prevention/what-are-common-symptoms-of-autoimmune-disease

Orenstein, B. W. (2022, December 19). *9 common digestive conditions from top to bottom*. Everyday Health. https://www.everydayhealth.com/digestive-health/common-digestive-conditions-from-top-bottom

Otsuka Pharmaceutical Co., Ltd. (n.d.). *Typical intestinal bacteria*. https://www.otsuka.co.jp/en/health-and-illness/fiber/for-body/intestinal-flora

Palmer, S. (2011). Is there a link between nutrition and autoimmune disease? *Today's Dietitian, 13(11), 36*. https://www.todaysdietitian.com/newarchives/110211p36.shtml

Paracelsus. (n.d.). *Paracelsus quotes*. BrainyQuote. https://www.brainyquote.com/quotes/paracelsus_170321

Pastor Guzman, I. (2020, January 18). *Are we what we eat?* Brain World. https://brainworldmagazine.com/are-we-what-we-eat

Patagonia Provisions. (n.d.). *The best (and worst) gut health foods*. https://www.patagoniaprovisions.com/blogs/learn/best-and-worst-foods-for-gut-health

Pelc, C. (2022, July 20). *Leaky gut and autoimmune disorders: Dormant "bad" gut bacteria may be key*. Medical News Today. https://www.medicalnewstoday.com/articles/leaky-gut-and-autoimmune-disorders-dormant-bad-gut-bacteria-may-be-key

Penn Medicine. (2022, March 31). *The truth about supplements: 5 things you should know*. https://www.pennmedicine.org/updates/blogs/health-and-wellness/2020/february/the-truth-about-supplements

Petre, A. (2020, January 10). *Is mustard good for you?* Healthline. https://www.healthline.com/nutrition/is-mustard-good-for-you

Petre, A. (2023, May 30). *AIP (autoimmune protocol) diet: A beginner's guide*. Healthline. https://www.healthline.com/nutrition/aip-diet-autoimmune-protocol-diet

Piedmont. (n.d.). *4 foods that help prevent chronic illness*. https://www.piedmont.org/living-better/4-foods-that-help-prevent-chronic-illness

Piedmont. (n.d.). *The health benefits of spicy foods*. https://www.piedmont.org/living-real-change/the-health-benefits-of-spicy-foods.

Pisharody, U. (2015, March 9). *The "leaky gut" hypothesis*. Swedish. https://blog.swedish.org/swedish-blog/the-leaky-gut-hypothesis

Pottle, Z. (2022, April 18). *Four best supplements for autoimmune diseases*. Pain Resource. https://painresource.com/supplements/supplements-for-autoimmune-diseases

Preiato, D. (2019, September 5). *What is marjoram? Benefits, side effects, and uses*. Healthline. https://www.healthline.com/nutrition/marjoram

Premier Health. (2021, November 10). *Avoid potential danger: Mixing medicines and supplements*. https://www.premierhealth.com/your-health/articles/women-wisdom-wellness-/avoid-potential-danger-mixing-medicines-and-supplements

Pristyn Care Team. (2021, August 21). *Drawbacks of allopathic medicines*. Pristyn Care. https://www.pristyncare.com/blog/drawbacks-of-allopathic-medicines-pc0113/

Probiotic-Digestive enzymes – Uses, side effects, and more. (n.d.). WebMD. https://www.webmd.com/drugs/2/drug-167708/probiotic-digestive-enzymes-oral

Public Health Agency of Canada. (2023, January 25). *Chronic disease risk factors*. Canada.ca. https://www.canada.ca/en/public-health/services/chronic-diseases/chronic-disease-risk-factors.html

Raman, R. (2023, February 1). *11 impressive health benefits of saffron*. Healthline. https://www.healthline.com/nutrition/saffron

Rath, L. (n.d.). *Inflammatory arthritis and gut health*. Arthritis Foundation. https://www.arthritis.org/health-wellness/about-arthritis/related-conditions/physical-effects/inflammatory-arthritis-and-gut-health

Regenerate Health Medical Center. (2023, April 13). *5 supplements for your autoimmune disease*. https://regeneratehealthmc.com/blog/5-supplements-for-your-autoimmune-disease

Robertson, R. (2023, April 3). *How does your gut microbiome impact your overall health?* Healthline. https://www.healthline.com/nutrition/gut-microbiome-and-health

Rocky Mountain Analytical. (2020, April 7). *Good vs. bad inflammation*. https://rmalab.com/good-vs-bad-inflammation

Roy, H. (2012). *Botanicals for health*. Pennington Biomedical Research Center. https://www.pbrc.edu/training-and-education/community-health-resources/pennington-nutrition-series/functional-foods/PNS_Botanicals_for_Health.pdf

Ruscio, M. (2021, August 27). *Meditation for IBS: Harnessing the gut-mind connection*. Dr. Ruscio. https://drruscio.com/meditation-for-ibs

Salko, E. (2022, January 21). *6 foods that worsen autoimmune disease*. Personalabs. https://www.personalabs.com/blog/6-foods-that-worsen-autoimmune-disease

Sampson, S. & Martin, K. (2021, October 14). *What to know about allopathic medicine*. https://www.medicalnewstoday.com/articles/allopathic-medicine

Sánchez, E., & Kelley, K. (2023, March 14). *Herb and spice history*. PennState Extension. https://extension.psu.edu/herb-and-spice-history

Santhakumar, S. (2022, February 23). *Western vs. Eastern medicine: What to know*. Medical News Today. https://www.medicalnewstoday.com/articles/western-vs-eastern-medicine

Sawhney, V. (2021, August 6). *Weirdly true: We are what we eat.* Harvard Business Review. https://hbr.org/2021/08/weirdly-true-we-are-what-we-eat

Scott, E. (2020, February 11). *How to practice loving kindness meditation.* Verywell Mind. https://www.verywellmind.com/how-to-practice-loving-kindness-meditation-3144786

Scott, E. (2021a, September 13). *Body scan meditation.* Verywell Mind. https://www.verywellmind.com/body-scan-meditation-why-and-how-3144782

Scott, E. (2021b, September 19). *Focused meditation: How to start a practice.* Verywell Mind. https://www.verywellmind.com/practice-focused-meditation-3144785

Scott, E. (2022, December 1). *What is mindfulness?* Verywell Mind. https://www.verywellmind.com/mindfulness-the-health-and-stress-relief-benefits-3145189

Sensoy, I. (2021). A review on the food digestion in the digestive tract and the used in vitro models. *Current Research in Food Science, 4*, 308–319. https://doi.org/10.1016/j.crfs.2021.04.004

Shapiro, S. (2017, September 5). *A mindful approach to chronic disease.* Genentech. https://www.gene.com/stories/a-mindful-approach-to-chronic-disease

Sharma, H. (2015). Meditation: Process and effects. *AYU (an International Quarterly Journal of Research in Ayurveda), 36*(3), 233–237. https://www.ncbi.nlm.nih.gov/pmc/articles/PMC4895748/

Sheridan, M. (2017, April 21). *"All disease begins in the gut." – Hippocrates.* HuffPost. https://www.huffpost.com/entry/all-disease-begins-in-the-gut-hippocrates_b_58f9ed4ee4b086ce58980fc3

Shmerling, R. H. (2020, October 27). *Autoimmune disease and stress: Is there a link?* Harvard Health Publishing. https://www.health.harvard.edu/blog/autoimmune-disease-and-stress-is-there-a-link-2018071114230

Shmerling, R. H. (2022, March 24). *Can vitamin D supplements prevent autoimmune disease?* Harvard Health Publishing. https://www.health.harvard.edu/blog/can-vitamin-d-supplements-prevent-autoimmune-disease-202203242712

Shreiner, A. B., Kao, J. Y., & Young, V. B. (2015). The gut microbiome in health and in disease. *Current Opinion in Gastroenterology, 31*(1), 69–75. https://doi.org/10.1097/mog.0000000000000139

The Silver Book. (n.d.). *Chronic disease.* https://www.silverbook.org/condition/chronic-disease

Sloat, S. (2021, November 22). *What is the gut?* Inverse. https://www.inverse.com/mind-body/what-is-the-gut

Smith, B. L. (2012). Inappropriate prescribing. *American Psychological Association, 43*(6), 36. https://www.apa.org/monitor/2012/06/prescribing

Smith, T., Morel, B., & Delgado, E. (2022, March 15). *Vitamins and minerals for pain management*. U.S. Pharmacist. https://www.uspharmacist.com/article/vitamins-and-minerals-for-pain-management

Snead, L. (2023, April 4). *Anti-inflammatory diet*. Johns Hopkins Medicine. https://www.hopkinsmedicine.org/health/wellness-and-prevention/anti-inflammatory-diet

Solan, M. (2021a, August 17). *The best foods for vitamins and minerals*. Staying Healthy, Harvard Health. https://www.health.harvard.edu/staying-healthy/the-best-foods-for-vitamins-and-minerals

Solan, M. (2021b, October 14). *Evoking calm: Practicing mindfulness in daily life helps*. Harvard Health. https://www.health.harvard.edu/blog/evoking-calm-practicing-mindfulness-in-daily-life-helps-202110142617

Sparks, Y., & Todd, M. (1997, December). Physical development: An overview. *Educational Psychology Interactive*. Valdosta, GA: Valdosta State University. http://www.edpsycinteractive.org/topics/physical-biology/physical.html

Spritzler, F. (2023, February 23). *10 supplements that fight inflammation*. Healthline. https://www.healthline.com/nutrition/6-anti-inflammatory-supplements

Starkman, E. (2023, July 8). *The autoimmune protocol diet?* WebMD. https://www.webmd.com/diet/autoimmune-protocol-diet

Stecher, C., Sullivan, M., & Huberty, J. (2021). Using personalized anchors to establish routine meditation practice with a mobile app: Randomized controlled trial (preprint). *JMIR MHealth and UHealth*, *9*(12). https://doi.org/10.2196/32794

Stojanovich, L., & Marisavljevich, D. (2008). Stress as a trigger for autoimmune disease. *Autoimmunity Reviews*, *7*(3), 209–213. https://pubmed.ncbi.nlm.nih.gov/18190880

Streit, L. (2019, July 25). *What is horseradish? Everything you need to know*. Healthline. https://www.healthline.com/nutrition/horseradish

Stromsnes, K., Garcia Correas, A., Lehmann, J., Gambini, J., & Olaso-Gonzalez, G. (2021). Anti-Inflammatory properties of diet: Role in healthy aging. *Biomedicines*, *9*(8), 922. https://doi.org/10.3390/biomedicines9080922

Stuart, A. (2023, May 9). *Colon cleanse: Is it good for my health?* WebMD. https://www.webmd.com/balance/natural-colon-cleansing-is-it-necessary

Subhadra, B. (2023, May 23). *10 warning signs you may have an unhealthy gut*. Biom Probiotics. https://biomprobiotics.com/10-warning-signs-you-may-have-an-unhealthy-gut

Summer savory – Uses, side effects, and more. (n.d.). WebMD. https://www.webmd.com/vitamins/ai/ingredientmono-684/summer-savory

Sun, Y., Ju, P., Xue, T., Ali, U., Cui, D., & Chen, J. (2023). Alteration of faecal microbiota balance related to long-term deep meditation. *General Psychiatry*, *36*(1). https://doi.org/10.1136/gpsych-2022-100893

Suttie, J. (2012, June 27). *Better eating through mindfulness*. Greater Good

Magazine. https://greatergood.berkeley.edu/article/item/better_eating_through_mindfulness

Szalay, J. (2023, January 20). *What is inflammation?* Live Science. https://www.livescience.com/52344-inflammation.html

Tabish, S. A. (2008). Complementary and alternative healthcare: Is it evidence-based? *International Journal of Health Sciences*, *2*(1), V–IX. https://www.ncbi.nlm.nih.gov/pmc/articles/PMC3068720

Tallon, M. (2020, April 13). *10 simple ways to practice mindfulness in our daily life.* Monique Tallon. https://moniquetallon.com/10-simple-ways-to-practice-mindfulness-in-our-daily-life

Tapsell, L. C., Hemphill, I., Cobiac, L., Sullivan, D. R., Fenech, M., Patch, C. S., Roodenrys, S., Keogh, J. B., Clifton, P. M., Williams, P. G., Fazio, V. A., & Inge, K. E. (2006, August 21). Health benefits of herbs and spices: the past, the present, the future. *Medical Journal of Australia*, *185*(S4), S1–S24. https://doi.org/10.5694/j.1326-5377.2006.tb00548.x

Temecula Center for Integrative Medicine. (2019, August 7). *Is the body designed to heal itself?* https://www.tcimedicine.com/post/is-the-body-designed-to-heal-itself

Todd, L. (2021, June 30). *10 of the healthiest herbs and spices and their health benefits.* Medical News Today. https://www.medicalnewstoday.com/articles/healthy-herbs-and-spices

Trecroci, D. (2022, March 25). *What is the difference between good gut bacteria and bad gut bacteria?* Pendulum. https://pendulumlife.com/blogs/news/what-is-the-difference-between-good-gut-bacteria-and-bad-gut-bacteria

Tsigalou, C., Konstantinidis, T., Paraschaki, A., Stavropoulou, E., Voidarou, C., & Bezirtzoglou, E. (2020). Mediterranean diet as a tool to combat inflammation and chronic diseases. An overview. *Biomedicines*, *8*(7), 201. https://doi.org/10.3390/biomedicines8070201

US Food and Drug Administration. (2022, June 2). *Mixing medications and dietary supplements can endanger your health.* https://www.fda.gov/consumers/consumer-updates/mixing-medications-and-dietary-supplements-can-endanger-your-health

US Forest Services. (n.d.). *Spices and herbs.* US Department of Agriculture. https://www.fs.usda.gov/wildflowers/ethnobotany/food/spices.shtml

UCLA Health. (2022, January 5). *When it comes to nutrition and chronic disease, focus on the basics.* https://www.uclahealth.org/news/when-it-comes-to-nutrition-and-chronic-disease-focus-on-the-basics

UCSF Health. (2023, May 8). *Top 10 foods for health.* https://www.ucsfhealth.org/education/top-ten-foods-for-health

The University of Queensland Australia. (n.d.). *Some common inflammatory diseases*. Institute for Molecular Bioscience. https://stories.uq.edu.au/imb/the-edge/inflammation/common-inflammatory-diseases/index.html

Vago, D. R., & Silbersweig, D. A. (2012). Self-awareness, self-regulation, and self-transcendence (S-ART): A framework for understanding the neurobiological mechanisms of mindfulness. *Frontiers in Human Neuroscience*, *6*. https://doi.org/10.3389/fnhum.2012.00296

Villalba, D. K., Lindsay, E. K., Marsland, A. L., Greco, C. M., Young, S., Brown, K. W., Smyth, J. M., Walsh, C. P., Gray, K., Chin, B., & Creswell, J. D. (2019). Mindfulness training and systemic low-grade inflammation in stressed community adults: Evidence from two randomized controlled trials. *PLOS ONE*, *14*(7). https://doi.org/10.1371/journal.pone.0219120

Vitamins can worsen autoimmune disease. (2021, September 26). Sun Sentinel. https://www.sun-sentinel.com/2008/08/13/vitamins-can-worsen-autoimmune-disease/

Vogel, K. (2022, August 5). *Can meditation help with pain relief?* Psych Central. https://psychcentral.com/health/meditation-for-pain-relief

Waldman, S. A., & Terzic, A. (2019). Health care evolves from reactive to proactive. *American Society for Clinical Pharmacology & Therapeutics*, *105*(1), 10–13. https://doi.org/10.1002/cpt.1295

Wartenberg, L., & Spritzler, F. (2023, May 23). *Anti-Inflammatory foods to eat: A full list*. Healthline. https://www.healthline.com/nutrition/13-anti-inflammatory-foods

Watson, S. (2023, September 13). *Everything to know about autoimmune diseases*. Healthline. https://www.healthline.com/health/autoimmune-disorders

WebMD Editorial Contributors. (2001, December 31). *Inflammation*. WebMD. https://www.webmd.com/arthritis/about-inflammation

WebMD Editorial Contributors. (2002, February 11). *Asthma*. WebMD. https://www.webmd.com/asthma/what-is-asthma

WebMD Editorial Contributors. (2003, January 23). *Type 1 diabetes*. WebMD. https://www.webmd.com/diabetes/type-1-diabetes

WebMD Editorial Contributors. (2004, July 8). *The digestive system*. WebMD. https://www.webmd.com/digestive-disorders/digestive-system

WebMD Editorial Contributors. (2020a, August 24). *Health benefits of basil*. WebMD. https://www.webmd.com/diet/health-benefits-basil

WebMD Editorial Contributors. (2020b, November 11). *Bay leaf: Health benefits, nutrition, and uses*. WebMD. https://www.webmd.com/diet/bay-leaf-health-benefits

WebMD Editorial Contributors. (2021a, April 8). *What is a balanced diet?* WebMD. https://www.webmd.com/diet/what-is-a-balanced-diet

WebMD Editorial Contributors. (2021b, June 15). *What is dysbiosis?* WebMD. https://www.webmd.com/digestive-disorders/what-is-dysbiosis

Welch, A. (2022, October 20). *How meditation can help manage chronic illness*. Everyday Health. https://www.everydayhealth.com/meditation/manage-illness

Welch, A. (2023a, January 17). *Meditation 101: A scientific guide on how to meditate for stress reduction and more*. Everyday Health. https://www.everydayhealth.com/meditation

Welch, A. (2023b, September 7). *How stress affects digestion*. Everyday Health. https://www.everydayhealth.com/wellness/united-states-of-stress/how-stress-affects-digestion

What is mindfulness? (n.d.). Headspace. https://www.headspace.com/mindfulness/mindfulness-101

White, A. (2023, May 15). *8 ways to do a natural colon cleanse at home*. Healthline. https://www.healthline.com/health/natural-colon-cleanse

White pepper – Uses, side effects, and more. (n.d.). WebMD. https://www.webmd.com/vitamins/ai/ingredientmono-1529/white-pepper

Whiteman, H. (2015, January 29). *Have we become too dependent on medication?* Medical News Today. https://www.medicalnewstoday.com/articles/288721

Whitlock, J. (2023, February 3). *The difference between chronic and acute conditions*. Verywell Health. https://www.verywellhealth.com/chronic-definition-3157059

Wigmore, A. (2019). *A quote by Ann Wigmore*. Goodreads. https://www.goodreads.com/quotes/563016-the-food-you-eat-can-be-either-the-safest-and

Williams, C. (2023, September 23). *The 8 worst foods to eat for inflammation*. EatingWell. https://www.eatingwell.com/article/2052349/the-8-worst-foods-to-eat-for-inflammation

Wilson, S. (2023, February 1). *The dangers of over-reliance on prescription medications*. WorldHealth. https://www.worldhealth.net/news/dangers-over-reliance-prescription-medications

Winston, D., & Smalley, S. (2023, March 27). *How to practice breathing meditation*. Mindful. https://www.mindful.org/how-to-practice-mindful-breathing

Witkamp, R. F., & van Norren, K. (2018). Let thy food be thy medicine.... when possible. *European Journal of Pharmacology*, *836*, 102–114. https://doi.org/10.1016/j.ejphar.2018.06.026

Wong, C. (2022, March 4). *Herbs for natural pain relief*. Verywell Health. https://www.verywellhealth.com/herbs-for-pain-management-89299

Wood, J. (2022, January 24). *Is the Western diet causing a spike in autoimmune diseases?* World Economic Forum. https://www.weforum.org/agenda/2022/01/autoimmune-diseases-western-diet-fast-food

Worst foods for digestion. (n.d.). WebMD. https://www.webmd.com/digestive-disorders/ss/slideshow-foods-to-avoid

Xiao, Q., Yue, C., He, W., & Yu, J. (2017, October 13). The mindful self: A mindfulness-enlightened self-view. *Frontiers in Psychology, 8.* https://doi.org/10.3389/fpsyg.2017.01752

Yang, Y. (2022, August 5). *Gut microbiome bacteria can evolve to cause autoimmune diseases.* Science in the News. https://sitn.hms.harvard.edu/flash/2022/gut-microbiome-bacteria-can-evolve-over-time-to-cause-autoimmune-diseases

You are what you eat: Why nutrition matters. (2016, July 25). Hospital News. https://hospitalnews.com/you-are-what-you-eat-why-nutrition-matters

Zamarripa, M. (2019, March 14). *6 surprising benefits of celery seeds.* Healthline. https://www.healthline.com/nutrition/celery-seed-benefits

Ziedman, E. (2022, May 8). *What are seed oils and should you avoid them?* Zero Acre. https://www.zeroacre.com/blog/seed-oils-to-avoid

Made in United States
Orlando, FL
08 January 2025

57030094R00114